940.54
TON

A WOR

Neil Tonge is a successful children's author steeped in a love of history. His books include a wide range to cater for all ages and tastes.

Townley Grammar School for Girls
Townley Road, Bexleyheath, Kent DA6 7AB

TOWNLEY GRAMMAR SCHOOL

R09753L0566

Also available from Macmillan

A WORLD IN FLAMES: AT SEA
Peter Hepplewhite

A WORLD IN FLAMES: CIVILIANS
Neil Tonge

A WORLD IN FLAMES: IN THE AIR
Peter Hepplewhite

A WORLD IN FLAMES
ON LAND

NEIL TONGE

Illustrations and maps by David Wyatt

MACMILLAN CHILDREN'S BOOKS

First published 2001 by Macmillan Children's Books
This edition produced 2002 by The Book People Ltd,
Hall Wood Avenue, Haydock, St Helens WA11 0UL

ISBN 0 330 48294 7

Text copyright © Neil Tonge 2001
Illustrations copyright © David Wyatt 2001

The right of Neil Tonge to be identified as the
author of this work has been asserted by him in accordance
with the Copyright, Designs and Patents Act 1988.

All rights reserved. No part of this publication may be
reproduced, stored in or introduced into a retrieval system, or
transmitted, in any form, or by any means (electronic, mechanical,
photocopying, recording or otherwise) without the prior written
permission of the publisher. Any person who does any unauthorized
act in relation to this publication may be liable to criminal prosecution
and civil claims for damages.

3 5 7 9 8 6 4 2

A CIP catalogue record for this book is available from the British Library.

Printed by Mackays of Chatham plc, Chatham, Kent.

This book is sold subject to the condition that it shall not,
by way of trade or otherwise, be lent, re-sold, hired out,
or otherwise circulated without the publisher's prior consent
in any form of binding or cover other than that in
which it is published and without a similar condition including
this condition being imposed on the subsequent purchaser.

CONTENTS

INTRODUCTION

On 1 September 1939, Germany invaded Poland. Britain and France warned the German dictator, Adolf Hitler, to withdraw his troops from that country within two days; otherwise they would declare war on Germany.

Hitler had no reason to believe them. So far they had given in to every one of his demands. First the Rhineland, then Austria and finally Czechoslovakia. Now it was the turn of Poland.

But this time he was wrong. On 3 September Britain and France declared war on Germany. There was little these allies of Poland could do, however, for they were hundreds of miles away and separated by Germany itself. Poland stood little chance against Hitler's massed tanks and the country was overrun within six weeks.

Britain sent its small Expeditionary Force to fight along-side the French but for eight months neither side launched attacks against one another. It was as if they were not at war at all. This brief period of calm before the storm broke in 1940 is often called the 'Phoney War'.

Hitler, however, was merely waiting for the best moment to strike. In May 1940 the German army launched a surprise attack in the mountainous region of the Ardennes, where the Allies were least expecting it. British and French forces were pushed back to the beaches of Dunkirk in a matter of weeks. An armada of ships, from pleasure boats to battleships, set out from Britain to rescue the remnants of the Allied armies. Over 200,000 British and 100,000 French were plucked from the jaws of the German **panzers** and brought safely back to England. France surrendered shortly afterwards, and Britain was left to fight on alone during what became her darkest days.

Success followed success for Hitler – until he made the fatal mistake of invading Russia in 1941. At last, Britain had an ally against fascist Germany and Italy.

Then what had only been a European war was transformed into a world war. Mussolini, the fascist dictator of Italy, dreamed of recreating the Roman Empire and launched campaigns in the Balkans and North Africa. He had little success and Hitler had to come to the rescue by strengthening his forces with German troops.

Later that same year, Japan made a surprise attack on the American pacific fleet. As a consequence, America declared war on Japan. Germany came to the help of her Asian ally and declared war on America. Further defeats followed for the British in Asia. Their colonies of Hong Kong, Singapore, Malaya and Burma fell to the Japanese until their forces were hammering on the gates of British India itself. But India did not fall.

1942 saw the first glimmerings of hope for the Allies. Slowly the tide was turning in their favour. In 1942, General Erwin Rommel, the hero of the German army, was defeated at the battle of El Alamein and his army pushed out of North Africa. In Russia, whole German battalions perished in the bitter cold or at the hands of the Russian army. In the Far East, the Japanese were gradually pushed back across the Pacific, and from Burma, to their homeland.

By 1944 the fascist countries of Germany, Italy and Japan were clearly losing the war. A second front was opened in Europe when the Allied armies landed in Normandy, France in June 1944. But as the Allies neared the frontiers of Germany, enemy resistance stiffened. It was to be one full year before the Allies entered the ruins of Berlin to find Hitler had taken his own life. In the Far East, the dropping of atomic bombs on two Japanese cities in August forced the Japanese to surrender.

There were thousands of individuals caught up in these powerful and extraordinary events. This book captures the stories of six people who were part of the history of a world in flames.

• In 1940, Private Ernie Leggett is one of the gallant

band of British soldiers who bear the brunt of the German onslaught on France. Badly wounded, he fears he will never see his home again.

• In 1942 the German army is 40 miles away from Cairo, Egypt. Bill Norris takes charge of a delivery of new Sherman tanks. Will they be enough to defeat the German general, Erwin Rommel, and his victorious Africa Korps?

• Parachuted behind enemy lines into occupied France in 1943, will Pearl Witherington, a brave Resistance fighter, evade capture and torture by the Gestapo?

• In June 1944 6,000 Allied ships lie off the coast of Normandy. Amongst the invasion force, Sergeant-Major Stan Hollis waits to lead his men into battle.

• October 1944. The Allied plan to shorten the war has gone disastrously wrong. Dr Graeme Warrack, captured by the Germans, decides to make a bid for freedom.

• In 1944 the 'Forgotten Army' of Burma is caught in a life and death struggle against Japanese forces. Gurkha rifleman Lachhiman Gurung stands alone against overwhelming odds.

RETREAT FROM HELL

BATTLE BRIEFING

On 1 September 1939 German forces attacked Poland, the ally of Great Britain and France. On 3 September, Neville Chamberlain, the British prime minister, warned the Germans to withdraw their army from Poland otherwise Britain and France would declare war. The Germans ignored this demand.

Cut off from Poland by Germany, there was little the Allies could do to help. The Polish army was no match for the lightning strikes of the German army. Polish cavalry made useless charges against German tanks. Heroically brave but badly equipped, they disintegrated within weeks and surrendered.

The Allies could have helped Poland by launching an attack in the west but very little happened. The British sent the BEF (British Expeditionary Force) of four divisions to join the 72 divisions of the French army but both armies needed to be trained and there was no plan for an invasion of

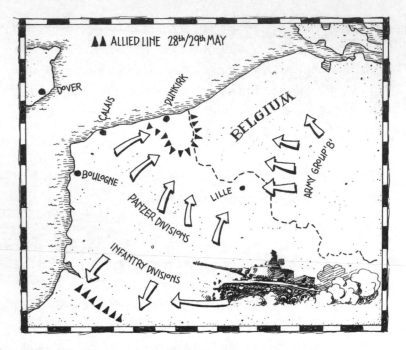

The Maginot Line.

Germany. Instead, they sheltered behind huge defence works called the Maginot Line, waiting for the Germans to destroy themselves on suicidal attacks at heavily defended positions.

At the end of the Polish campaign Hitler ordered his generals to prepare for an autumn attack against the Allies in the west. Bad weather and advice from his general, however, persuaded Hitler to change his mind and wait for the spring.

As dawn broke on 10 May 1940, the Germans unleashed their terror. Instead of attacking the Maginot Line they simply went around it. Drawing the Allied armies into Belgium and

6

Holland, their main thrust was further south in the wooded and hilly area known as the Ardennes. Spearheaded by tanks and dive-bombers, the German army sliced the Allied armies in two, sending the British Expeditionary Force and part of the French army reeling back to the coast of France. Private Ernie Leggett was amongst the retreating British soldiers.

Date: 10 May 1940 onwards
Place: Orchies, near Lille, northern France
A Sudden Awakening

Private Ernie Leggett pulled the blankets tightly round his neck and snuggled deeper into the warmth of the bed. 'No hurry to be up and about in this strange kind of war,' he thought to himself. 'Just the sort of soldiering I like – no shooting and lots of fun in la belle France.'

Most of his mates thought the same way. They were sick of the war before it had even started. They wanted to go home and did not give a bean for a faraway people in Poland and a strange-sounding city called Danzig. Besides, Ernie had heard someone say that it was all Germans that lived in the city anyway, so why the fuss? If only Hitler would stop stirring things up they could all go home.

Ernie turned on to his other side and stretched. 'May as well go home – not a German to be seen and all we do is march and drill all day long.' Glowing coals in the hearth and a singing kettle on the range filled Ernie's mind. He longed for home, for his little village of

Clippersby. And it was true. The tiny BEF and their French allies had done little more than stare at one other since September of last year.

A few pamphlets had been dropped on Germany warning them that they would lose the war, although it was difficult to see how this could be achieved with bits of paper. True, the French had advanced into Germany – all of five miles! And occasionally they fired a few rounds at the Germans from the safety of the Maginot Line. With the memory of 1.3 million men dead from the 1914–18 war fresh in every Frenchman's mind it was understandable that there was no enthusiasm to rush to war.

Without warning the door was nearly shaken from its hinges by a furious knock. Ernie, drifting back into sleep, was jolted awake. 'What the——?' he cursed as he pulled the blankets aside and peered outside. Company Sergeant Major Gristock was in the middle of the Rue de la Gare bellowing out instructions for the men to 'fall-in'.

Ernie tumbled out of the door, pulling his battledress jacket tight but leaving his shirt tail streaming out behind him. In the distance, he caught the sound of the muffled boom of heavy artillery fire coming from the direction of Lille. The sky was the usual steel-grey of early morning but at the airfield bases, less than ten miles away, the sky was glowing a smoky red and plumes of oily smoke were curling up into the sky.

One hundred and twenty men of the 2nd Battalion, Royal Norfolk Regiment, tumbled into the streets of Orchies where they had been billeted.

'Attention!' Sergeant Gristock barked out the command and seconds later every man had snapped to attention.

'Get your kits, we're moving out – NOW!'

Within minutes the men had grabbed their equipment, including one or two 'unofficial' bottles of wine. They were barely a mile from their billets when several black specks appeared in the morning light. Screaming from the sky, German bombers flew low over Orchies. Several muffled explosions could be heard as the bombs detonated and clouds of dusty smoke billowed up and spread like a dirty curtain over the houses. Minutes before and the men would have been buried under the rubble.

Climbing out of the ditches where they had taken shelter, they patted the dust from their uniforms and hurried to the safety of the wood. Ernie had been born and bred in the countryside and knew how to read the signs that nature left as warnings. Not a bird was singing. Rabbits scuttled for cover.

He loved the countryside but he also loved the army. He was young and healthy and had joined as a boy soldier at 16. As well as learning infantry drill, he had been trained to play the drums in the Regimental band. Dressed in the ceremonial dress of leopard-skin and watching the men keep step to the beats of his drum filled him with enormous pride.

He was proud too that from his princely wages of 10 shillings per week he could send money home to his mother. Even prouder that he was highly regarded as an expert marksman with both rifle and **Bren** gun. It came naturally to him. He and his brother had hunted rabbits as soon as they were old enough to hold a gun.

Once under cover of the woods the soldiers settled down to brewing tea, smoking cigarettes, thinking of home and wondering what was in store for them. What would their orders be? Would they be in the thick of the fighting?

Ernie leaned against the thick trunk of an oak tree and looked up at the dappled sunlight through the canopy of trees. He was anxious. What he feared most of all was losing his nerve. Shaming himself in front of his mates. He felt he would not let anyone down but there was one thing that made him squirm more than anything else.

Bayonets! He winced at the thought. They'd been taught how to use one. It all sounded so mechanical. 'Push it in, twist it and then rip it out.' And they'd practised on stuffed dummies, screaming at the straw effigies in order to screw up their courage. But the thought of doing it to another human being or, worse still, have the enemy do it to you, made his blood run cold.

The Plan

Daylight faded into night. Captain Barclay and some of

the sergeants told the men to gather round. In the pale light of hurricane lamps, the officers began to explain what they were to do.

Captain Barclay cleared his throat. 'The Germans are pouring over the frontier. Our duty is to stop them. We will be crossing into Belgium, which is under attack. There we will pick up our motor transport and head for the front.

'Now, men, it only remains for me to tell you that our "holiday" is over. Now, more than ever, your training will stand you in good stead. Keep your heads down and your spirits high, and from now on when you aim your rifle to shoot, you shoot to kill.'

Forming up in silent columns, they set off in the evening gloom, approaching the Belgian frontier by small back roads. They reached their lorries without incident and headed in the direction of the enemy. Progress was slow, for the roads were flooded with refugees. Bicycles, old prams, any wheeled transport that would carry their meagre possessions, filled the roads to bursting point. Heads were bent in dejection; children's faces stained with tears.

Stuka Attack

Stranded in the slow-moving streams of desperate civilians, the soldiers became easy targets for the Stuka dive-bombers. The German pilots dived from towering heights, spraying machine-gun bullets and dropping bombs into the midst of the terrified groups of people.

Bundles of clothing were left scattered on the roadside as the refugees ran for cover.

Ernie and the others tumbled out of the back of the lorries and rolled into the ditches. The Stuka bombers were terrifying. Sirens were fitted to their wheels and there were whistles on the bombs so that they sounded like a tribe of monstrous banshees raging in the skies. Ernie shook like a jelly.

Company Sergeant Major Gristock ordered the men to pull themselves together and to 'get fell in'. But when he thought they weren't looking, he cast an anxious eye towards the skies. 'Where are the "boys in blue" when you most need them?' he thought to himself. They hadn't seen any sign of the RAF all day.

In Full Retreat

The onslaught of the German advance could not be halted and the BEF found itself fighting rearguard actions as it retreated through Belgium and back into France. Grim evidence of their defeat was everywhere. Bodies lay by the roadside. Burnt-out shells of lorries and motorcycles lay like charred skeletons across the road. Abandoned artillery guns pointed forlornly to the sky. And everywhere there were signs of panic as soldiers had dropped their equipment to ease their escape. Terrified refugees streamed through the litter of defeat, making troop movement almost impossible.

But discipline had remained tight in Ernie Leggett's

battalion during their four-day retreat. Orders arrived for them to form a defensive line along the river Escaut, where a German attack was expected any hour. Taking cover in a cement factory, Ernie and his comrades could look out to woods on the opposite bank from the balconies that jutted out from the building. Even though there was no sign of movement, they knew the Germans must be over there. Dragging tables and boxes to the balconies, the soldiers barricaded the windows and doors and set up their Bren guns to give a broad sweep of the woods and far embankment. Ammunition was stacked and ready and sentries were posted. Ernie wrapped himself in his army blanket and tried to get some sleep. Despite the hard floor, he was soon fast asleep, exhausted by the days spent in retreat.

Under Attack

The sunlight streamed in through the windows and woke Ernie from his deep sleep. He rubbed his eyes and joined the corporal who was peering at the woods opposite. An eerie silence hung over the woods. No birds sang and even the river seemed uncannily still. A low moaning wind swept through the long grass.

As Ernie and the corporal scanned the far bank for signs of the enemy, they spotted several German officers talking and pointing to the factory. Seconds later, squads of soldiers appeared at the edge of the woods, hauling boats down to the water.

A rush of excitement coursed through Ernie's body.

The moment of truth had finally arrived. Ernie raised his rifle and took aim.

The corporal raised his arm and placed it on the barrel of Ernie's rifle. 'No, not yet. Captain Barclay will give the signal. We'll catch them on the move.'

The Germans clambered down the bank. They must have known that the British were on the opposite bank but this did not deter them from carrying out their orders.

Captain Barclay was fearless and had an odd way of showing it. He carried a hunting horn wherever he went, which he used to signal orders to his men. Captain Barclay placed it to his lips and sounded the attack. A volley of rifle fire crashed from the British line. German soldiers dropped where they stood or scattered for the limited cover that lined the river bank.

Ernie took careful aim. His chosen target, a German crawling down to the canal. Ernie squeezed the trigger gently, the man jerked suddenly and then stopped moving.

The corporal turned to Ernie and gave him an approving smile. 'Here! Take this for a while.'

The corporal handed the stock of the section Bren gun to Ernie who fitted it into the crook of his shoulder. Before he could fire, Private May, lying on the other side of Ernie, gave a grunt and fell forward. A small trickle of blood ran down his forehead from an ugly hole in his temple.

Ernie whispered the Lord's Prayer as the Bren gun

stuttered into action. Machine-guns and mortars opened up from the opposite bank. Half-track vehicles crashed through the undergrowth and perched on the embankment, opening up a steady fire on the cement factory.

'Thy will be done . . .' Ernie continued to mouth the prayer, summoning courage from the repetition of the familiar words. Bullets were flying everywhere. The Bren gun juddered as it spat bullets out at the German soldiers still making their way down to the canal and it took Ernie all his strength to aim it accurately. By this time all the men were shouting out their own prayers and oaths – most of it sheer nonsense.

Spent shell cases clinked across the concrete floor as Ernie fired the gun in short bursts. German soldiers spun backward from the impact of his bullets or juddered as they fell into the long grass and bushes of the river bank.

There was very little cover for the German attackers and panic was beginning to set in. At last they broke and retreated to the cover of the woods.

'Cease fire!' Captain Barclay's orders boomed out and the rifle fire fell silent. Once again the low moan of the wind could be heard through the long grass. In the moment's silence that followed, it dawned on Ernie and his comrades that they had defeated the enemy attack. A muffled cheer rang out, echoing around the blood-stained walls and floor.

By mid-afternoon on 21 May the Germans had pin-pointed the positions of the British soldiers and were picking them off with sniper fire. Two had already been killed and one was carried downstairs screaming. Ernie had tried to block out the sound.

The situation was steadily getting worse. The corporal had been killed, picked out by a sniper as he tried to remove the over-heated barrel of the Bren gun. Worst of all, the mortars were slowly but inevitably blasting the walls of the factory to pieces. The section was now down to four men but those that remained hung on to their positions grimly.

Ernie peered out of the balcony and saw an English soldier crawling towards the river over open ground. He was working his way closer and closer to a machine-gun nest. What the soldier did not realize and could not see was that the Germans were setting up a second machine-gun position close by.

Springing up from the long grass, the English soldier lobbed a grenade at the first machine-gunners, shooting them with his rifle as they scattered for cover. But he was now in full view of the other machine-gun and stood no chance. The second machine-gunners swung round their weapon and in a swift burst of gunfire cut the man down. Ernie could not see who it was but learned later that it was their own Company Sergeant Major George Gristock. The CSM died of his wounds and was later awarded the Victoria Cross for his bravery on that day.

Ernie had little time to take in what he had seen before a mortar bomb crashed in through the smashed roof. Ernie was sent spinning through the air, hitting the ceiling and landing with a dull thud. A pool of blood slowly spread out from beneath his body.

Two of Ernie's comrades raced to his side. Ripping the trousers from his legs, they exposed a savage wound in Ernie's groin. If it had severed his main artery he was finished. He would be dead within a minute. But Ernie's mates were not going to give up on him. Plugging the huge hole with field dressings, they tied the whole bundle together with a tourniquet. Ernie was carried downstairs and gently placed in an outhouse where they left him. He was unaware of all of this for he had fallen unconscious. When he woke up, he knew that he must make it back to their headquarters, otherwise he might well die or get left behind.

He struggled to his feet and immediately fell over. He would have to crawl. A railway line at the back of the factory offered meagre cover but it was all there was. He dragged his half-naked body along. A trail of blood marked his route. He lost consciousness once more.

I must have passed out because the next thing I felt was my wrists being pulled. And I looked up into the faces of two men who I knew well. They were both clarinet players in the band. And they said 'It's Ernie.'

And as I faded into unconsciousness again I heard one say to the other, 'He's had it.'

But Ernie had not 'had it'. Bundled aboard a 15-hundred weight truck he was bumped, jostled and jolted all the way back to Dunkirk. The doctors had injected him with morphine to deaden the pain. Ernie was confused during this time. At times he thought he was still travelling to the front to fight Germans, at others walking around St Peter's Church in his own village of Clippersby. Evacuated from Dunkirk on a hospital ship, he eventually arrived back in Blighty. Only then did he feel safe and rested and could confidently say, 'Thank God I'm home.'

Ernie is still living, although the wound that he received that day still twinges and aches. And every Remembrance Day, Ernie plays the bugle in honour of all those not as fortunate as himself who did not make it home but lie in a grave in France.

1939 – The 'Phoney' War

Unbelievably, the British and French did little to come to the aid of Poland, preferring to wait for the Germans to attack them. For nearly eight months they simply stood and stared at one another.

The Germans cynically called this period of the war *sitzkrieg* or 'sitting war' – so unlike the *blitzkrieg*, or 'lightning war', that they had unleashed against Poland and were soon to unleash on France.

FIGHTING FACTS

Tanks 1940

	Max. Speed (mph)	Weight (tons)	Number available	Number in crew
France				
Somua S35	25	20	260	3
Renault R35	12.5	9.8	950	2
Char B1	17.5	32	311	4
Hotchkiss H35	17.5	11.5	545	2
Hotchkiss H39	22.5	12	276	2
Britain				
Matilda MkII	15	26.5	75	4
A10	18	14	126	5
A13	30	14	30	4
Germany				
PzKwII	16	9	1095	3
PzKwIII	25	19.3	388	5
PzKw 38(t)	26	9.7	410	4
PzKw 35(t)	25	10.5	273	4
PzKwIV	18.5	17.3	278	5

Gordon Waterfield, British war correspondent for a daily newspaper, was disgusted by the attitude of the British army:

Across the river a young German was standing in the sun, naked to the waist, washing himself. It annoyed me that it should be possible for him to go on washing calmly there with two machine-guns facing him on the opposite bank. I asked the sentry why he did not fire. He seemed surprised at my bloodthirstiness and said, 'We are not wicked and besides, if we fire they will only fire back at us.'

Blitzkrieg Terror

The Germans had perfected a new kind of warfare called *blitzkrieg*. Air attacks were blended with massed tank units and motorized infantry. This meant that the Germany army could punch holes in the enemy's defences and move in fast to surround them. During the battle for France some of the tank units covered as much as 40–60 miles a day. Curiously, both British and French military writers had recommended *blitzkrieg* tactics but only the Germans had put them into practice.

Exhaustion

During the retreat to Dunkirk few soldiers had time to rest, let alone sleep, but the 1st East Surrey battalion finally invented a way to doze a little on the march. By linking arms, two outside men could walk a man between them as he slept. From time to time they'd switch places with one another.

Belgium's Surrender

The Germans quickly overran Belgium. When the Belgians surrendered they left a huge gap in the British and French armies, which had to be quickly plugged.

One Belgian officer refused to obey the order and set off for the French lines. Staying in the war was not as easy as he thought, however. A French sentry accused him of being a traitor and a coward and warned that he would shoot him if he came any closer. Turned back, he made his way to the British lines. They were afraid that he might be a spy and refused to let him through. Eventually, joining up with other Belgians he boarded a fishing boat and made for England.

Saved by the Panzers

The Germans too were exhausted by the speed of their advance and stopped to rest on Hitler's orders, reassured by Goering that he could finish the British and French off with his **Luftwaffe**. Hitler ordered a further halt. This gave a valuable two days in which the British could arrange for the remnants of their army to escape from Dunkirk back to England.

Heinz Guderian, commander of the Panzer Tank army, was amazed at the decision. 'We were utterly speechless. Just over the horizon lay Dunkirk. The BEF could have been destroyed on the beaches.'

Dunkirk – Defeat or Victory?

Between 24 May and 3 June 1941 over 200,000 British and over 100,000 French soldiers were evacuated to Britain, leaving the Allies with an army to continue the fight against Nazi Germany.

British troops on the beaches of Dunkirk, under attack
from the German Luftwaffe.

The Grim Reality

British Expeditionary Casualties	68,111 killed, wounded or taken prisoner
Equipment abandoned	Artillery guns 2, 472 Rifles 90,000 Vehicles 63,879 Motorcycles 20,548 Stores and Ammunition 500,000 tons
Ships Sunk at Dunkirk	243 out of 860
Aircraft Lost	474

A painting of the scene
at Dunkirk.

The Hope

Troops evacuated 338,226 (139,097 French)
These remained the only
trained troops left to defend
Britain but they were without most of their equipment.

What Saved the British?

The weather. The English Channel rarely stays calm but for nine days during the evacuation of Dunkirk the sea remained like a millpond.

• Overhead mists and rain seemed to come at the right moment. The Luftwaffe mounted three assaults on

Dunkirk and each time low cloud prevented a follow-up.

• Hitler's order of 24 May, halting his tanks just as they were closing in for the kill.

• Herman Goering announcing that the Luftwaffe alone could deal with the French and British armies.

• The determination of the British to rescue their army and the thousands of volunteers who brought their boats into the dangerous waters.

DESERT
DUEL

BATTLE BRIEFING

Following the fall of France in May 1940, the Italian dictator Mussolini allied his country with Germany. This agreement between the dictators of Germany and Italy became the so-called 'Pact of Steel'. In reality, Italy was entirely dependent on its victorious neighbour north of the Alps.

This did not prevent Mussolini, however, from trying to prove that his country could be just as successful in military campaigns as Germany. Dreaming of the creation of a new Roman Empire in the Mediterranean, the Italian army invaded Greece, only to have the adventure end in embarrassing stalemate. Germany was forced to come to their rescue and conquer Greece.

In September 1941, Mussolini decided on another campaign. Crossing the frontier wire from their colony Cyrenaica, in North Africa, the Italians attacked the British in Egypt, at that time part of the British Empire. The small but well-trained British forces stopped them in their tracks and pushed them all the way back to Benghazi.

Again Germany was forced to bale out her ineffective ally. In 1941, Hitler especially chose one of his top generals, Erwin Rommel, to command this combined force of Italians and Germans (Axis powers) and strengthened their punch with three panzer (tank) divisions. This had an immediate and dramatic effect.

The Axis forces pushed the British back into Egypt and were soon poised to strike at Cairo and the Suez Canal. This would have secured the huge Middle Eastern oil reserves for Germany and cut Britain's link with India and her Empire in the Far East. The situation was perilous.

In July 1942, the Germans began to batter at the British defences at El Alamein, the last defensible line before Cairo. At this most dangerous moment the Germans were beaten back, suffering heavy losses.

The British now turned to the attack but each offensive quickly got bogged down. Both sides felt the stalemate couldn't continue and the British were desperate for a victory.

In defiant mood, but privately anxious, Winston Churchill, the British Prime Minister, visited Egypt on 5 August. He wished to encourage the troops by his presence but also to assess the situation for himself. Churchill decided a change at the top was necessary. General Auchinleck was relieved of his command and replaced by the somewhat eccentric General Bernard Montgomery.

Montgomery was a perfectionist in his military duties but a rather lonely and arrogant commander. Many soldiers of the Eighth Army, however, saw his arrogance as a sign that he had confidence in his ability to win battles, and he soon inspired considerable trust. He toured all the divisions within his army and gave simple but inspiring speeches to the men, often from the bonnet of his jeep.

He would not go into battle until he was absolutely ready. Churchill kept demanding action but Montgomery insisted that victory would not happen until he had built up sufficient resources and his battle plan had been perfected.

Throughout September 1942 the Germans attempted to break through the British defensive lines but they held fast. On 23 September, Rommel fell ill and was flown home on sick leave. This misfortune for the Axis forces was to assist the British.

On 23 October 1942, Montgomery launched his long-anticipated attack. Bill Norris was a commander of one of his tanks.

Date: 23 October– 4 November 1942
Place: The Western Desert, Egypt

Tank Command

Bill Norris sank back into the luxury of a bath brimming with hot, soapy water. It had been a long time since he felt he could relax. After being chased by Rommel's forces thousands of miles across the desert and eating when and what he could, Bill was enjoying this moment

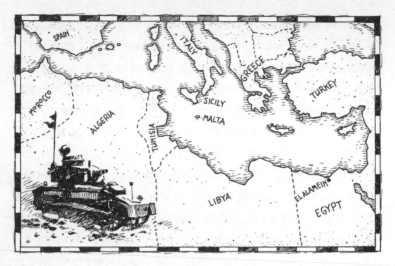

North Africa.

away from the battlefield. They'd all taken a real mauling and were in a sorry state. The order had then gone out to prepare a defensive line at El Alamein – less than a day's march from the Suez Canal. If the German tanks made a breakthrough they would be finished. 'Still,' Bill thought to himself, 'we've got a new commander. Spindly blighter, this Monty chap, but very sure of himself.'

But for a few brief moments he could forget all these things for there were more treats in store – real food and a real bed! Bill smiled to himself. It wasn't just the luxuries he was now enjoying that pleased him but the reason he'd been sent to Alexandria in the first place. 'At last,' he thought, 'we have a tank which will settle the enemy. We've been out-gunned by the Germans for too long. It's true they're tough, not like the Italians, but they're not unbeatable. And now we've got the tank that's going to even things up!'

Bill had been sent to the port of Alexandria in Egypt to take delivery of eighteen gleaming monsters. The Sherman tank, manufactured in America, was a good match for the German tanks. It was thirty tons of 3-inch armour plating, bristling with a magnificent 75 mm turret gun and three machine-guns and could roar into battle at 25 mph. He couldn't wait to see the men's faces when they saw their new weapon.

Jumping Off

'Tomorrow . . . tomorrow's the day.' The order for the next day flashed around the Eight Army like a terrible secret that needed to be whispered. But there was little time for the men to dwell on their personal thoughts for much had to be done. Ammunition, rations and fuel had to be checked and loaded aboard. Crews had to become familiar with their new Sherman tanks.

By early evening all was ready. At 21:40 precisely on 23 October, a furious Allied barrage of 882 guns lit the night sky with so many rounds fired that it seemed as if daylight had come early that morning. The ground trembled and the air vibrated. Bombers droned overhead and the bombs crashed like thunder. Four infantry divisions with fixed bayonets advanced. Moonlight glinted on their weapons.

The order was given for Bill's tanks to move to their

An artillery barrage lights the night sky.

jumping-off position in front of the minefields, which they reached the following day. And there, in the shimmering heat of the desert, was their objective. There were very few recognizable locations in the desert, but opposite them was a crumbling ridge, casting a dark shadow over the surrounding wasteland. This was their target.

Smoky dusk settled over the desert and then vanished into the blue-blackness of night. Bill and his crew were waiting for the order to advance once a path through the minefields had been cleared. He admired the men who did this, who risked death and terrible injury every day. It was their job to find the mines and dig them up. Every metre of terrain had to be cleared by gingerly prodding the sand with a bayonet, for only a few of them had mine-detectors and they weren't always very effective. The steel had to be kept at about a thirty-degree angle – any steeper and the mine could detonate. Some mines were booby-trapped and the slightest pressure on their surface would detonate them. Often trip wires linked several mines together and when one was removed it detonated the others, usually with fatal consequences but sometimes leaving a crippling injury to arm, foot or leg.

In this rare moment of calm before a battle, Bill surveyed his crew. His wireless operator had died during the last battle with the Germans. He'd been sitting alongside Bill on the turret of the tank when a red-hot shell splinter pierced his upper arm and lanced straight into his heart. It was almost impossible to use the periscope accurately and at least one man, the commander or one of his crew, usually had his head protruding from the top, directing the fight. This made him a sitting target.

Bill's new wireless operator was a ladies' hairdresser from London and the crew boasted the best haircuts in the regiment. He was also a superlative cook and a genius at transforming bully beef and hard biscuits into meals that at least looked edible.

Bill's gunner was an Irishman. The driver was a giant

blond Norwegian, who'd escaped from his country after the Germans had invaded. Because of his massive height he was nicknamed 'Tiny'. And what strength! He once broke a track on a tank by heaving at the steering wheel too hard. The second driver was Jewish. He never got into a 'spin' in battle but calmly worked away at firing the machine-gun. They were good people to have around. Despite being from so many different backgrounds, they were bound together in their hatred of the Nazis.

Into the Storm of Battle

By the evening of the 24th a ten-mile path had been cleared through the minefield and Bill's tank crew could advance on the enemy. Light reconnaissance Crusader tanks led the way, followed by heavier Grants and finally Bill's beloved Shermans. Two searchlight beams lit either side of the track to prevent the Allied tanks straying into uncleared minefields.

Bill looked up into the heavens. The stars appeared no more than tiny, twinkling dots of light. The moon was bright and silvered the tanks as they crawled at a snail's pace towards the enemy lines. Fortunately, there was no wind but the thousands of vehicles on the move churned up so much dust that the drivers were unable to see ahead and relied on instructions from the commanders sitting above the turrets of the tanks.

Ahead of Bill and the tanks the Allied bomber planes were at work. Flashes streaked the sky, whilst red mushroom clouds of flames billowed into the night when a fuel or ammunition dump was hit.

Suddenly, by some strange coincidence all the engines stalled, except for one lone Crusader which ploughed on, perilously alone. It then pulled up and towed a tank behind it, managing to get it started again. One by one the tanks gradually re-started. Bill cursed. For a moment they had been sitting targets. Fortunately the Germans had not responded.

As dawn silvered the horizon, they were clear of the minefields and heading down a long reverse slope towards their objective at the top of the ridge. As they climbed the track, they passed the burnt-out shells of a regiment of Shermans, all knocked out by anti-tank guns. They'd been caught as they were silhouetted on top of the ridge by the setting sun the previous night.

Enemy locations were spotted up ahead and the tank commanders took sightings through their binoculars and directed the fire. Some German shells caused a few casualties but after the pounding they received from the Allies, they began to withdraw to second line defences.

As Bill began to appreciate the pause in the battle, a tank to his left suddenly exploded, the turret shooting twenty feet into the air. At first, it was thought that a stray shell from the fleeing enemy had hit it until the blackened faces of the tank crew crawled from the wreckage.

'Stupid stoves,' they mouthed in exasperation. Bill's

crew smiled, knowing too well the dangers of the little petrol stoves they were equipped with to make a 'brew-up' for tea. They'd blown themselves up!

As they waited for their orders, a group of about 100 German prisoners, fingers laced together and held on top of their heads, filed past the tanks. They got no further. A gunner in one of the Shermans opened fire at them and the prisoners crumpled, screaming, before dying of their wounds. Before the gunner could extend his field of fire, the machine-gun was wrestled from his hands and he was dragged from the vehicle. Bill learned later that the gunner's brother had been killed in a previous engagement and the soldier could think of nothing but revenge. He was taken into custody and Bill never saw him again.

That night the tanks were corralled in a circle like a wagon train expecting an Indian attack. The infantry dug in around the perimeter. This was the most dangerous of times, for enemy infantry often filtered through tank lines and opened fire.

Turning the Tide of War

The battle boiled on for several days. The men could scarcely keep awake and snatched what little sleep they could. Bill and his men were at the centre of the battle-field but most of the action was taking place to the north where, after heavy losses, the Allies began to force the Germans into retreat. Rommel, who had returned to the front, although still ill, gave orders for a withdrawal.

Now was the moment to throw the enemy off

balance. Bill and his fellow tank commanders raced in a north-westerly direction to begin to surround and cut off the enemy. But they were too late, for Rommel and the Afrika Corps were already beginning to flee back along the coast road, abandoning masses of equipment in their hurried retreat.

And then, as if the Germans had won an ally in the weather, the rains came on 1 November. Any thought of rapid pursuit became bogged down in the winter rains.

Bill surveyed the wreckage of battle. As the rain pattered down upon the desert sands, tiny flowers began to bloom in their millions. And with the rains, the victory at El Alamein turned the tide of war when Montgomery launched Operation Supercharge on 2 November, which began to outflank the Axis forces. In Britain, church bells,

Wounded British soldiers await an
Advanced Dressing Station.

which had remained silent and were only to be rung if a German invasion took place, pealed out in victory.

The fighting was far from over but, as Churchill said, El Alamein was, 'Not the end, not even the beginning of the end but the end of the beginning of the war.' Before, Bill had hoped for victory – El Alamein proved it was possible. Rommel, despite his reputation, could be outfought. Britain now had a general who rivalled that of the Germans.

FIGHTING FACTS

Naming the Battle

El Alamein took its name from a lonely railway station just over a mile from the coast. The Allied defensive line stretched from this railway station some 40 miles to the south where it ended at the Quatra Depression, a huge range of hills surrounding a vast bowl of treacherous sand. No vehicle could travel through this southerly area so there was no danger that the Germans could circle behind the Eighth Army.

The Duelists

Bernard Law Montgomery was born the son of a bishop in 1887 and spent his youth in Tasmania, Australia, before his family moved to England. Not a very popular student at Sandhurst, the military college for officers, he made his mark through hard work. On the Western Front in World War I he won the Distinguished Service Order for bravery.

Montgomery had the reputation of being an eccentric, although he was a perfectionist when carrying out his military duties. Despite writing a book on infantry tactics, his promotion was slow before the war. His appointment as a commander of the battered Eighth Army in August 1942 was to prove a turning point in his career, however, and in the British army's campaign. His victory over the Axis forces made him a hero and he was honoured with the title of Viscount Montgomery of Alamein, although his men affectionately called him Monty.

Erwin Rommel was born in 1891 the son of a schoolteacher. In World War I he was so determined to win the Order of Merit he led his men into very ferocious fighting and he won the award.

After war ended he came to the attention of his army superiors as an inspiring teacher of tactics. His lectures were published in a book on infantry tactics. It was a best-seller and its fame brought him to the attention of Hitler. Rommel believed in Nazi ideals and lived only for his army career. When war broke out he was given command of a panzer division and played a major part in the fall of France.

Later, when the Italians were sent reeling in North

Africa by the Allies, Rommel was sent to stiffen resistance. He soon won new successes, driving the British forces back to Egypt. Fortunately for the Allies he became ill and was flown back to Germany whilst Montgomery built up his own forces for attack. Flying back to take command, Rommel fought a fierce battle at El Alamein but because his supply lines were so long he was forced to retreat. Nevertheless, he managed to withdraw his forces without capture.

Hitler, not wanting him to be tarnished with defeat, brought him back to Europe where he was put in charge of preparing the defences in France against an expected Allied invasion. After the Allies landed, Rommel became increasingly convinced that Germany would lose the war and was implicated in a plot against Hitler. As a Field-Marshall in the German army, Hitler did not want Rommel's disloyalty to be widely known so as a consequence he was given the option of committing suicide. Backed into a corner, Rommel chose to take his own life.

The Sherman Tank

The arrival of the American Sherman Tank in the deserts of North Africa came as a nasty shock to the German panzer crews. Bill collected one of the 252 tanks delivered to the Eighth Army in time for the battle of El Alamein. It was fast moving and had high firepower. Despite the brief breakdown of Bill's Sherman tanks at

El Alamein, it was magnificently reliable and mechanically efficient. By 1944, however, it was no match for the German Tiger and Panther tanks.

Facts about the Sherman

Weight	32 tons
Speed	24 mph
Armour	76 mm steel front
	56 mm steel side
Weapons	MkV 75 mm gun
	Penetration 74 mm of armour at 100 yards

Enemy Tanks

The Panzer IV was the most numerously produced German tank of the war. By 1944 it had passed its best but it was still a formidable opponent.

Facts about the Panzer Mark IV

Weight	25 tons
Speed	25 mph
Armour	80 mm front armour
	30 mm side armour
Weapons	75 mm gun could penetrate 99 mm of armour at 100 yards

Battle Strengths at El Alamein

	Axis Forces	Allied Forces
Aircraft	350	530
Tanks	489	1,029
Soldiers	104,000	195,000
Artillery	1,219	2,311

We Were Only Looking!

Two important Italian officers were captured by the Allies in the desert by a reconnaissance patrol. Brought back to headquarters for interrogation they complained bitterly that they had not taken part in any battle, they had only been observing British methods. The fact that they were enemies did not seem to strike either of them as strange and, as one of the angry pair announced, 'This is an absolute outrage. We were only looking!'

Desert Rats

It may seem strange for a soldier to want to be nick-named a 'rat', a name that conjures up dirt and filth or, when it's applied to a human being, someone who can't be trusted. But desert rats are a different type of rat altogether. They are clean, can bound along fast on long back legs and, above all, can live in the harsh conditions of the desert. For these reasons, soldiers of the Eighth Army were only too proud to be honoured by the nick-name of 'desert rats'.

RESISTANCE

BATTLE BRIEFING

People in countries occupied by the Germans had a difficult choice. They could try to get on with things as they were and work with the new government and armed forces, becoming collaborators. Or they could resist by passing on information about German troop movements or blowing up trains carrying enemy troops. To resist, of course, was highly dangerous.

A few brave men and women joined resistance groups but the German secret police were highly efficient and many resistors were killed or captured. No mercy was shown to prisoners, who were usually tortured before being executed.

Soon after the fall of France, resistance groups began to appear all over Europe but they were badly organized and were frequently destroyed. Britain quickly realized, however, the value of the military information these groups provided and began to parachute agents into occupied France.

41

Occupied Europe and North Africa.

These agents had to be alert at all times. Often tiny things betrayed them. One agent was arrested because he was looking for oncoming traffic in the direction he was used to in Britain.

From 1941 onwards the British and American Secret Services played an important role in organizing these secret armies, and women were in the forefront. They fought with machine-guns and grenades alongside their male comrades in the French Resistance.

As the Germans began to lose the war more and more people joined the Resistance movements. In remoter parts of France, small armies called the Maquis were formed, which did much to disrupt German troop movements when the Allies landed on the Normandy coast. Pearl Witherington was one of these brave fighters.

Date: 23 September 1943
Place: RAF Tempsford airfield, Bedfordshire

Night Flight

Pearl Witherington studied the sky as the gloom gathered around the secret airfield at RAF Tempsford in Bedfordshire. Hedged between the Great North road and the main railway line from London to Edinburgh, few flights took off from its concrete runways. For this reason, most passing visitors, as well as the locals themselves, dismissed this base as unimportant.

They were wrong to do so. In fact, Tempsford was one of the main bases from which RAF Special Duties sent secret agents into the heart of Nazi-occupied France. The journey was perilous, and particularly so in the fragile Lysanders and plodding Halifax aircraft. If they were not caught in the searchlights and flak (anti-aircraft fire) then the agents themselves could well be parachuting into a trap set by the Germans, having been betrayed by the people they had been sent to help.

Pearl understood the dangers only too well, for she had already escaped from France once before. Trapped in Paris by the unexpected speed of the German advance, Pearl and her parents and three sisters had no intention of 'sitting out' the war. As the German radio broadcast news of devastating bombing raids by the Luftwaffe on London in the autumn of 1940, the Witheringtons decided to make their bid for freedom.

To England

The first stage of their journey was to cross into the unoccupied area of France. The north and the Atlantic coastline were garrisoned by German troops. To the south and east, the French were allowed to set up a puppet government, answerable to their German masters. Marshall Petain, a World War I general, was brought out of retirement to head the collaborationist state of Vichy, named after the town which became its capital.

To cross the demarcation line was dangerous. Every French person had to carry a pass stamped by the Germans giving them permission to travel. All trains, cars and lorries were searched. Forging passes became a major industry from which fortunes could be made. It was a perilous trade. If caught, the guilty could expect long prison sentences.

Pearl, a secretary in the British embassy, managed to get papers and tickets to Marseilles in the unoccupied zone of France but it took just about all her family's savings. Arriving hungry and penniless in Marseilles, they hoped to get passage aboard a Red Cross ship back to England but the ship never came. Meanwhile, Pearl kept her family in whatever food was available. Horsemeat and lungs were frequently on the menu, being the cheapest cuts of meat.

Crossing the Pyrenees

Pearl was not the sort of woman to sit and wait for things to happen. She persuaded the rest of the family that as the Red Cross ship was unlikely to arrive, their only alternative was to cross the Pyrenees into neutral Spain. They made their way to Gibraltar, a British colony, and found room on a troopship returning from Egypt.

On 14 July 1941 they sailed into Glasgow. Determined to enlist in the forces as soon as they landed, Pearl's two younger sisters, Mimi and Jackie, immediately joined the WAAF (Women's Auxiliary Air Force). But before their training could begin, the newspapers got hold of their story. They became immediate celebrities, having run great risks to get back to England to serve their country. 'They Walked a Thousand Miles to join the WAAF' trumpeted the headlines.

Pearl was pleased but was content to remain in the background and obtained a humdrum job at the Air Ministry. But after the excitement of their daring escape, Pearl soon grew bored with the routine work of a secretary. Hearing vague rumours about secret operations in France, Pearl went to her boss and volunteered. Such work was 'hush-hush', however, and Peal was refused permission. Secret Operations preferred to make their own approach and sometimes in odd ways.

Undeterred, Pearl made further inquiries and learned that there was an office at 82 Baker Street that had something to do with the Secret Operations group. As a secret organization it was careful not to advertise its presence. Situated down a narrow alley, the door plaque simply stated, 'Inter-Services Research Bureau'.

Volunteer for Danger

Pearl braced herself and marched in. On the top floor, a tall man with thinning hair offered her a seat and let her speak without interruption. Pearl did not know it at the time but this was no other than Colonel Maurice Buckmaster, head of Special Operations Executive, F section (F for French).

Pearl spoke with passion of her hatred of the Nazi conquerors and she did so in fluent French. When she had finished, Buckmaster held out his hand. 'Thank you, Miss Witherington. This has been a most interesting interview. I will be in touch.'

Several weeks later, as Pearl began to think she'd been forgotten, she received a call. She was to report to Wanborough Manor, where she was put through a tough mental and physical training programme. Agents were not released into France unless their trainers were convinced they would survive. They had to live, breathe, eat and think as French people. Woken up in the middle of the night, they had to remember to reply in French and not English.

After five months of gruelling training Pearl was ready

to return to France. She could say nothing to her family about her destination and they simply had to accept that she had gone missing 'on duty'.

To France

The Halifax bomber was waiting for her, purring on the runway. She checked her equipment and heard a 'good luck' coming from the shadows as her trainer wished her well. She turned and climbed into the small Hillman truck that would take her across the airfield to the looming shadow of her transport aircraft. She felt the night close in around her. She was alone, utterly alone and there was no turning back.

There were no comforts in the Halifax bomber. It was not designed with that in mind. Pearl tried to settle down for the journey ahead into occupied Europe but the noisy aircraft constantly vibrated, and it was freezing cold. The engine roared as it tried to pick up enough revs for take-off. At 125 miles per hour, the aircraft lurched into the air, as Pearl's stomach flipped over.

Pearl had been given an important mission. She was to be second in command to Squadron Leader Maurice Southgate who had been entrusted with a vast area of France stretching from the Loire to the Pyrenees. A number of armed Maquis resistance fighters were operating in this area and their underground war against the Germans needed coordinating. Pearl and Maurice already knew one another from when they had both been employed in the Air Ministry. It was an ideal partnership, for they both liked and respected one another. Pearl was not to know, however, that Maurice had a special assignment in mind for her.

The shuddering bomber flew low over France, picking its route carefully to avoid main towns where it would attract anti-aircraft fire. The navigator checked his calculations by glancing through the aircraft windows, looking for recognizable rivers glinting in the moonlight and the dark shadows of hill ranges and mountains.

Pearl heard the shuffling creak of a leather flying jacket as one of the aircrew made his way along the fuselage towards her. 'Miss Witherington, soon be over the drop zone. We've got you safely there. Just came to check your gear,' he said cheerfully, hoping that his good spirits would fill Pearl with confidence. He pulled at her webbing and harness, making sure it was secure, before clipping her to the static line that stretched the length of the fuselage. This would automatically open Pearl's parachute as soon as she jumped.

He tapped her on the shoulder, a beaming smile on his lips as he gave her a reassuring thumbs-up. Turning his back to her, he wrestled the exit door open. A blast of cold air rushed into the cabin and Pearl stared out into the star-pricked sky.

A red light flashed above the door, flickered for a few moments, then turned to green.

'Go!' snapped the RAF officer.

Pearl jumped before she had time to think about what she was doing. She hurtled away from the Halifax and safety into the silent night sky. The parachute flapped open and soon she was sailing down towards blotches of trees and open fields.

As she raced towards the ground, shadows ran from clumps of bushes towards her. Could they be German? She peered into the dark, trying to distinguish whether the figures were wearing steel helmets. As she thumped to the ground the figures reached out for her, pulling the silk of the parachute to one side.

'Pearl . . . Pearl, it's me Maurice.' Maurice's strong embrace raised her to her feet. 'Come on! We can't hang around here.'

The Reunion

Maurice bundled her into a car and, taking little back roads, they arrived at a farmhouse in the next district. As the door opened, the warm light that bathed the parlour dazzled Pearl. She blinked. She could scarcely believe what she saw. A man strode towards her, his face split by a broad smile and his arms held wide to hug her.

'Henri . . . Henri Cornioley! How can it be? You were taken by the Germans.' Pearl was puzzled but delighted that her childhood friend was free and there in the room.

'Pearl. How have you been? What's a nice girl like you doing mixing with dangerous people like us?' he joked.

Henri explained what had happened to him since they

had last met. After escaping from a German prisoner of war camp, he'd joined the French Resistance. Now they were to work together.

The Maquis

Pearl's first task was a difficult one. The French colonel who commanded the local Maquis group was a stubborn individual. His men were in desperate need of reorganization and re-equipping but he wanted things to stay as they always had been. Pearl went to work on him with all her charm. One hour later he was agreeing with her, two hours later and he was giving orders in line with Pearl's wishes.

Pearl worked tirelessly throughout the winter months of 1943 giving recruits weapon-training, planting explosives on railway lines and organizing receptions in drop zones.

All agents had to be suspicious of anyone and everyone. They could not afford to relax for a moment and this put a tremendous strain on them. It took only a brief lapse of concentration and an agent could fall into the hands of the Gestapo – the German secret police. On 1 May disaster struck.

Maurice made his fatal mistake on that hot day. Maybe he was tired from the heat or constantly being on his guard. Whatever the reason, his mistake was costly. Dashing to the house of a wireless operator in Paris, he forgot to check whether the 'all clear' signal was in place – a towel hanging from the windowsill. Maurice burst into the room and straight into the arms of the Gestapo. Punched and jostled, he was handcuffed and marched off to their headquarters. But despite rough treatment, torture and imprisonment he survived.

Pearl was left in sole command of Maurice's operations and at a particularly crucial time. The Germans knew by the increased bombardment of railway lines and by wireless messages that an Allied invasion was about to take place, but they were not sure where it would be. As a precaution, they began to step up their raids on suspicious houses.

Pearl narrowly escaped arrest herself when she was bounding up the stairs to a contact's house. She'd reached the first landing when a loud hiss stopped her in her tracks. 'Come down,' the caretaker of the building mouthed to her. 'The Gestapo are waiting for you.'

Night after night, Pearl ordered her 3,000 Maquis fighters into action. The main Paris railway line was cut several times. Telephone and telegraph wires were blown up or cut. Soon the Germans put a price on her head, offering one million francs for her capture. Posters showing her picture and detailing the reward were plastered all over the region.

On 5 June, the Maquis began to fight German troops in the open, drawing their soldiers away from Normandy, where the Allies were to land. Many Frenchmen were killed in these skirmishes. On one occasion, 11 June,

Pearl and 150 French resistance fighters were surrounded by 2,500 German soldiers. At one point in the fire fight, Pearl was trapped in a cornfield. The Germans sprayed their bullets everywhere but, miraculously, Pearl wriggled on her belly out of danger. As she recalled:

I had to be very careful how I moved. I watched the heads of the corn above me and as the breeze stirred them I moved a little closer to the edge of the field. I had to wait until the wind moved the corn, otherwise the Boche would have noticed it moving and fired directly at that spot. But they finally gave up and I managed to get away.

Honouring a Hero

In the middle of September 1944 Pearl's region of France had been liberated and she handed over command of her Resistance group to a French officer. Her force had been responsible for the deaths of 1,000 German soldiers and the capture of a further 20,000.

When she returned to England it would have been expected that she should have received the highest honour in the land. Indeed, she was recommended for the Military Cross but objections were raised because this honour was for men not for women. In a 'man's world', no one could imagine that a woman could have such startling bravery. Instead, Pearl was sent the MBE (Medal of the British Empire) Civil, which was a medal given to civilians for acts of bravery. Pearl sent it back. A few weeks later, she was offered another MBE but this time in recognition of her military exploits.

This, however, is not quite the end of the story. Shortly before the war ended, Pearl married her childhood sweetheart, Henri Cornioley and went to live in Paris, in the country which they had done much to help liberate.

FIGHTING FACTS

The Results of Resistance

Intelligence information

By the end of the war Allied intelligence information was excellent. It came from a number of sources.

Resistance groups throughout Europe had painstakingly built up networks of contacts, which gave information about German troop positions and movements.

Early in the war British agents captured a German coding machine, called an Enigma, from a German U-boat. The Germans thought their codes were unbreakable but they were wrong. As a result masses of battle orders became known to the Allies throughout the war. This information was distributed to the Allied commanders and leaders under the code name 'Ultra'. The British wished to keep their source of information secret so that the Germans would not change their coding machines. Some 'Ultra' information was of very high quality, including some of Hitler's operational orders.

An Enigma code machine.

Deception

The Allies' attempts to fool the Germans had some notable successes. In one instance an actor played the part of General Montgomery, and once a dead body was dumped in the Mediterranean Sea with false plans for the invasion of Europe in his pockets. 'Fortitude', the plan to disguise Allied landings in Normandy, achieved 100 per cent success.

Other deceptions included reports that General Patton, a famous American general, was touring a mythical invasion army in England. And plans for an invasion of Norway kept German forces scattered all over Europe. Even when the Allies finally landed in Normandy, Hitler refused to give orders for reserves to be committed to the battle, as he believed the landings themselves were a deception.

Escape

The British helped to set up escape lines, particularly to bring back aircrews who had been shot down. By 1944, for every airman captured an equal number was assisted back home. At that time it cost up to £15,000 to train a single fighter pilot and £23,000 to train the seven-man crew of a Lancaster bomber. In today's figures, the cost of training a fighter pilot would be approximately £500,000. Britain needed those men!

In all, 33,517 people in the armed forces returned from enemy-held territory during the war. Out of these 23,208 escaped. Most of these escapees were aircrew.

Sabotage

Factory sabotage in occupied countries made a large dent in the German war effort. Agents in France carried out about 150 attacks on French factories, mines and power installations. In few cases did they bring production to a full stop, however. Probably the most important raid by resistance fighters was in Rjukan, in Norway, when a German plant making materials for an atomic bomb was effectively knocked out.

Results of sabotage on a train carrying
German troops, 30 July 1943.

Attacks on troops

Isolated attacks often brought savage reprisals from the
German and Italian armies. When Heydrich, the commander of German intelligence in Czechoslovakia, was
assassinated, orders were given for all the inhabitants of
the village of Lidice to be massacred. In France a similar
massacre occurred at Oradour sur Glane.

However, there is no doubt that the **partisans** in
Russia kept many German soldiers on occupation
duties, and the rising of the French resistance fighters –
the Maquis – in France kept German divisions busy.

The Stress of Being an Agent

Secret agents were under enormous pressure not to

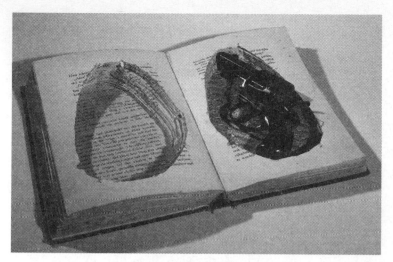
Book with a hiding place for a pistol.

betray themselves or their comrades. The slightest drop in their guard could give them away. Surprisingly, when Maurice Southgate was arrested he remembers a sense of relief, thinking, 'At last I can sleep.'

Plastic Explosives

In 1943 a new weapon was dropped to resistance groups. Plastic explosive was safe to carry around and could produce the same destructive results as several heavy bombers. This meant they could be even more effective in their sabotage of German troops.

Charles de Gaulle

Charles de Gaulle, a French army officer, set up the Free

French Forces in 1940 in order to continue fighting against Germany. They fought with the Allies in Africa, Italy and France. By 1944 there were more than 300,000 regular troops, and the Resistance had acknowledged de Gaulle's leadership. De Gaulle became a national hero, and the symbol for a free France, after entering Paris in triumph on 26 August 1944.

Collaborators

In Norway the Germans put a collaborator called Quisling in power. He tried to change school history books in line with Nazi ideas. Every history teacher in Norway refused to teach from the new books and was arrested. Eventually, because the prisons became so crowded they had to be released.

The Plot to Kill Hitler

Resistance in Germany was even more dangerous. In 1944 a plot to kill Hitler nearly succeeded. Lieutenant Colonel Count von Stauffenberg planted a bomb under the planning table at Hitler's headquarters in East Prussia. It was accidentally pushed further under the table, however, so that when it exploded Hitler was partly shielded. This saved his life. Thousands were arrested after this incident and hundreds, including von Stauffenberg, were executed.

D-DAY: DELIVERANCE OF EUROPE

THE NORMANDY INVASION: 6 JUNE 1944

As dawn broke on 6 June 1944, 6,000 Allied ships lay off the coast of Normandy in the biggest ever sea-borne invasion. Overhead, thousands of British and American aircraft swarmed over the French coastline to pound the enemy's defences, whilst airborne troops parachuted behind German lines to cause havoc and disruption.

It was one of the best-kept secrets of the war and security was tight. The Germans were convinced that the invasion would take place at the narrowest stretch of the channel – the Pas de Calais, opposite the English port of Dover. The Allies did all they could to make the Germans think they were right. Dummy landing craft were stationed all the way along the River Thames. Radio signals gave the impression that a force was being assembled for this destination. Five weeks after the D-day landings, the Germans were still convinced that the Normandy landings were a decoy to throw them off the scent.

That day, 250,000 soldiers stormed ashore along a 60-mile stretch of well-defended beaches. They faced formidable obstacles. Field Marshall von Runsted, the German commander responsible for the defence of France, Belgium and Holland, had more than half a million men under his command for the task. The beaches were packed with clever death traps to kill and maim an invading army. Every 1,000 metres, concrete pillboxes bristled with anti-tank guns, flame-throwers and machine-guns, manned by 50 to 200 men.

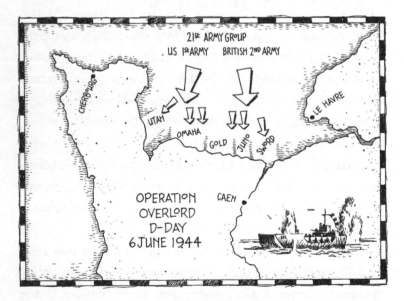

Operation Overlord.

Further inland, gun batteries were built to pound troop ships, whilst panzer divisions waited to spring on the Allies and throw them back into the sea should they break through.

Amongst those that hit the beaches on that longest of days was Company Sergeant Major Stan Hollis of the 6th battalion The Green Howards, a famous regiment in the British army. This is the story of what happened to one man on that fateful day.

Date: 6 June 1944
Place: Gold Beach, Normandy, France

As Dawn Breaks

Sergeant Stan Hollis took a quick look round at the men of D company who packed the landing craft. Bullets whined overhead and thumped into the side of the boat. Aircraft droned overhead. Artillery fire stabbed the sky. Oily smoke plumed from burning wrecks and caught in the back of the soldiers' throats.

As each man faced the likelihood of a sudden and violent death, most retreated into their private thoughts and fears. Some prayed silently, others thought of their families or tried to control their trembling. Many were seasick and longed for the land – no matter what it would bring.

The Landing Craft Assault bucked wildly in the swell of the sea. Water swept over the bows, but between the showers of spray that stung the eyes the thin, grey coastline of France gradually emerged into recognizable

Troops loading a landing craft aboard a ship.

buildings and clumps of trees. This was what all their training had been leading to. The aerial photographs that Stan and his men had studied for months were now taking shape before their eyes. From the edge of the beach, a thin track ran up to a house with a circular drive and beyond to the rise of a hill where their main objective lay – the gun battery at Mont Fleury. Their view then disappeared into the haze of open country.

Amazingly, they were right on target. As the LCA closed in on the shore, Stan was aware of an unsettling and eerie silence. The roar of shells from the bombarding ships offshore had fallen silent and, as yet, the German defences were not replying. He knew that this was only a lull and once the Germans returned to their guns all hell would break out. He could not shake one thought from his mind. The photographs had revealed what looked like a pillbox on the sea wall. It was well sited. From its vantage point it could send a deadly arc of fire along the beach.

'They need to be kept busy or my boys will be slaughtered,' Stan thought to himself. Taking a machine-gun from one of the men he balanced the weapon on the ramp of the landing craft and sent several bursts of fire in the general direction of the pillbox. The lurching of the landing craft made aiming difficult but he hoped that it would at least persuade the Germans to keep their heads down. As the craft neared the beach, Stan cupped his hand beneath the barrel to support its weight, quite forgetting in the tension of the moment that the barrel would still be hot. A searing burn printed itself across the palm of his hand.

'My first wound in this battle and it's self-inflicted. Sometimes you forget the most obvious things in the "heat" of battle.' He smiled wryly to himself at his own joke but at least it had the positive effect of calming some of his fears.

The landing craft hit the beach with a jolt, throwing a few of the men off balance. The ramp crashed down and the men piled out. They were soon waist-deep in ice-cold water. Weighted down with equipment, some fell face down into the water and drowned.

Stan snapped into action. Followed by three machine-gunners and three mortar-men, he raced for the high water mark, where his squad were supposed to lay down a smoke-screen to cover the rest of the soldiers as they scrambled up the beach. There was no need. Exploding bombs had already created an oily curtain of smoke that hung in strands across the beach.

British troops landing on a beach in Normandy.

Looking back to the shoreline, Stan kept his eye on the remaining landing craft. One driver had driven his vehicle with such force at the shore that its nose had become securely stuck in the sand. As the driver pressed harder on the accelerator to free the vehicle it had the opposite effect. Instead of forcing itself free, the tail began to swing round – straight towards a mine attached to a pole. The ramp should have come down when the vehicle hit the beach but this did not happen. Instead, the men were frozen in the safety of their metal shell.

At great personal risk, Stan jumped to his feet. He knew his voice would not carry above the din of battle but nevertheless he shouted to them, whilst waving his arms in a frenzy of warning. At first it had no effect. The tail was spinning ever nearer to destruction.

Only inches from the mine, however, one of the crew woke from his frozen state and gave the ramp a violent kick. Down it crashed and the men tumbled out, racing up to the ridge of sand that marked the high water limit.

There was no time to stop. The ridge of sand only gave temporary safety. Stan waved his men on. They must not become stranded on the beach. To do so would only allow the Germans to counter-attack and throw them back into the sea. But they needed to break through a line of hedge and bramble that ran parallel to the beach. Once through this obstacle they could then storm their main objective: the Mont Fleury gun battery.

Stan squirmed through a gap in the hedge and, emerging on the other side, he headed for the house with the circular drive. A burst of automatic fire crashed out from the area of the house and two men close to him fell wounded.

First Action

Stan gritted his teeth. 'Unless these guns are silenced,' he thought, 'the rest of D company has no chance of destroying the Mont Fleury battery. They'll be shot in the back!'

Stan, accompanied by Major Ronnie Lofthouse, crept up to the wall that surrounded the house, whilst two platoons raced past up the track to open the assault on the Mont Fleury battery. Major Lofthouse inched his head above the wall and spotted the source of the fire. A field gun was just visible amongst the bushes. The Germans had now turned their gun so that it was firing at the two platoons.

'There's a pillbox in there, Sergeant Major.' Major Lofthouse pointed to a clump of bushes about fifty metres to the right, just beyond the end of the wall.

Without waiting for further orders, Stan took off in a frontal assault on the enemy position. The Germans swung the gun round and began opening fire on him. Stan tried to weave and dart to make himself a difficult target. Bullets kicked up spurts of dust all around him but, miraculously, none of them hit him. Within seconds, he had reached the concrete wall and, without pausing,

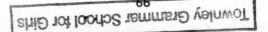
Townley Grammar School for Girls

pushed the muzzle of his gun through the firing slit, spraying bullets into the black interior. Then he scrambled on to the top of the pillbox, lay down, unpinned a grenade and 'posted' it through the firing slit. A muffled bang was followed by a cloud of dust blown out of the metal door at the back entrance of the pillbox. Jumping down into the trench at the rear, he burst through the door. Two dead Germans were sprawled across the dirt floor, whilst the others, too dazed or wounded to put up any further resistance, surrendered.

British commandos push ashore.

Emerging back into the sunlight, Stan noticed that the trench he was in ran on for a further 100 metres, which led to another pillbox. He snapped another magazine into his Sten gun and advanced cautiously along the trench. As he approached the remaining pillbox the German defenders poured out. He stopped and pointed the muzzle of his gun at the bewildered Germans. His determined stance persuaded them that further resistance was useless and they put their hands up in surrender.

A few moments later, Sergeant Hollis reappeared on the track, leading a line of 25–30 prisoners, which he shepherded towards the beach patrols.

Meanwhile, the battery at Mont Fleury had taken such a heavy pounding that the German defenders had decided to abandon their position. As the Allied troops began to move further inland, however, German resistance began to pick up and a number of officers and men were killed. When Lieutenant Kirkpatrick was shot, Platoon 16 became leaderless and CSM Stan Hollis was ordered to assume command.

The Farmhouse

By mid-afternoon, D company had reached the village of Crepon and was pushing beyond en route for Bayeux. To the left of the main road from the village an old stone farmhouse dominated the route inland.

'An excellent place for snipers to hide,' thought Stan, 'but dangerous to clear. Sensitive trigger fingers could kill or wound my men as rooms are searched and doors kicked open.'

Stealthily, Stan's platoon set about searching the house, moving cautiously from one room to the next. The sergeant's ears were alert to the slightest sound and he was convinced that he heard a trickle of loose plaster hit the floor in one room. Bursting into the room, his gun was cocked to fire. He expected to be met by gunfire but the huddled shape he saw in the corner was too small to be a soldier. The figure turned its head and two frightened eyes stared at the sergeant. Stan pulled up his gun and gave the boy a toothy grin. A less experienced soldier might not have taken the chance but Stan would have found it impossible to live with himself if he had killed this innocent boy.

Not satisfied with merely clearing the farmhouse, Stan began to search the rest of the farm to ensure that no Germans were in hiding to wreak havoc behind the British lines. He had a healthy respect for the German soldier. Most were brave; some were fanatical and would willingly lay down their lives for the Fatherland. Stan moved gingerly down an alleyway at the back of the farm and, just as he was about to turn the corner, there was a loud crack of rifle fire. A bullet just missed the end of his nose and gouged out a piece of masonry centimetres from his face.

Stan fell flat on the ground and scanned the hedge ahead. About fifty metres away, a couple of dogs were wagging their tails and jumping around near a gap in the leafy cover. 'They can't be doing that without a reason. There must be someone there that the dogs have got used to,' reasoned Stan, 'and that must be the German gunners.'

Stan raced back to the road where he collected a **PIAT** anti-tank gun and ordered two Bren gunners to follow him. Meanwhile, the rest of his command was to draw the Germans' fire from the opposite direction.

Stan fell flat on his stomach and crawled through a patch of rhubarb to get a good sighting of the field gun. He took aim. But no covering fire erupted to distract the field gun. All his men had been wounded or killed by an alert enemy, but he was not to know this at the time. He opened fire but, to his horror, the round fell short. The Germans were now alerted to the sergeant's attack and turned their field gun in his direction. He could clearly see the black hole of the muzzle pointing directly at him, less than one hundred metres away.

Then there was a shattering explosion which deafened him. Seconds before, he had closed his eyes, expecting to die, but instead, the shell whistled over his head and slammed into the house behind him.

'To hell with this; I'm getting out of here.' Shouting to the two Bren gunners to follow him, Stan crawled back through the rhubarb patch to the cover of the wall. Reaching the road and D company, he reported back to Major Lofthouse, who decided that as the gun was no immediate threat to the operation it could be safely left to be 'mopped-up' by another patrol.

Their conversation was interrupted by the sound of machine-gun fire from the farmhouse. Stan looked around for the two Bren gunners and then realized to his horror that they had not heard him and had been left behind at the farmhouse. Snatching a Bren gun for himself, he sprinted back along the alleyway that ran alongside the wall. Reaching the end, he did not stop to take cover but raced into the orchard, shooting from the hip and screaming at the two men to get out. He stopped about fifty metres from the field gun, springing bullets in that direction until the two Bren gunners could make a hurried retreat. Miraculously, none of them were harmed.

The 6th Green Howards continued their advance until, as night began to fall, a halt was called. Sergeant Hollis slumped to the ground, loosened the straps of his helmet and pushed it back from his forehead. He ran through the actions of the day in his mind; his own narrow escapes from death, and remembered those who had not been so lucky. What he did not know was that he had been recommended for the highest honour in the British army – the Victoria Cross – the only soldier to be so decorated on D-day.

Company Sergeant Major Stan Hollis survived the war and many years later returned to the farmhouse where he had carried out his heroic action. To his great surprise the ten-year old boy, Monsieur Lahaye, was now the owner of the farm. Having shared that terrible moment of war, they greeted each other as long-lost friends.

FIGHTING FACTS

After D-Day the Allies began to force the Germans to retreat from their occupied territories. This marked the beginning of the end of the war.

The Atlantic Wall
After 1942, when the tide of war was beginning to turn against Germany, Hitler gave orders for concrete defences to be built along the European coast. The toughest defences were placed along the Pas de Calais. Field Marshal Rommel was placed in charge and was not impressed with what he found. In some cases the Germans had only erected balsa screens propped up by concrete walls to trick the Allies!

Fooling the Enemy
The Allies knew they had more chance of winning if they could fool the Germans into thinking they were going to land elsewhere. Operation Fortitude was the plan to persuade the Germans that the Allies were going to land at the nearest point to England – the Pas de Calais. A fic-

Rommel inspecting part of the Atlantic Wall.

titious army was created in Scotland to suggest that
Norway might be invaded. More fictitious armies were
created with dummy tanks and landing craft mushroom-
ing along the banks of the river Thames.

The code name for the invasion of Normandy was
Operation Overlord and Operation Neptune was the
code name for the naval assault. Petrol was to be supplied through an underwater pipeline from England –
Operation Pluto. There were also code names for the
five groups of forces landing on the beaches – Utah,
Omaha, Gold, Juno and Sword.

Imagine the horror of the D-Day planners when a
crossword appeared in the *Daily Telegraph* containing the
words 'Pluto', 'Overlord' and 'Omaha'! The crossword

compiler received a visit from the Secret Service but, they concluded, it had been no more than a frightening coincidence.

The Invasion Force
Throughout May 1944 the south of England became one huge military camp.

Operation Overlord D- Day 6 June 1944

Troops

	Infantry Divisions	Armoured Divisions	Airborne Divisions	Total per country
United States	13	5	2	20
British	8	4	2	14
Canadian		1		1
French		1		1
Polish		1		1
Total	21	12	4	37

Air Forces
Heavy Bombers	3,958
Medium and light	1,234
Fighter bombers	<u>4,709</u>
	9,901

Naval Forces
Battleships	7
Monitors	2
Cruisers	23
Gunboats	2
Destroyers	93

Sloops	15
Escorts	<u>142</u>
	284

| Landing Craft | 4,308 |

Special Type Equipment

LVTs	470
DD Tanks	514
DUKWs	<u>2,583</u>
	3,567

Officers and Men

Air	659,554
Land	1,931,885
Sea	<u>285,000</u>
	2,876,439

Pinned on the Beach

Five groups landed on the beaches. Only on Omaha beach did the Allies experience real difficulties, with 1,000 dead and 2,000 wounded.

Bob Edlin, an American infantryman, was at Omaha beach:

I saw one of the sergeants there and his left thumb was gone but he didn't look as if he was hurt too badly so I called his name and told him to get up and come with us. But when I got closer I saw there was blood all

over his back . . . and then I was hit by machine-gun
fire in the left leg and the pain was terrible. It knocked
me down and I thought, 'Well, I haven't been here ten
minutes and I've already got a Purple Heart.'

Inventions That Won the Day

Operation Mulberry

The raid on Dieppe in 1943 had made it clear that it would not be easy to capture an undamaged port. To solve this particular problem over one hundred giant concrete blocks were towed across the channel and positioned off Gold and Omaha beaches to form artificial harbours.

Operation Pluto

The problem of how to supply petrol was solved with underground supply lines.

Many other inventions were designed to make the invasion a success. Tanks were fitted with giant flails at the front to explode mines.

Weapons That Won the Beaches

P-51 Mustang fighter plane

This made an important contribution to the successful Normandy landings by winning air control from Germany. It was one of the most remarkable aircraft of the war. It was capable of flying to Berlin and back with long-range drop tanks and out-gunning every Luftwaffe

Aerial view of Mulberry harbour.

opponent. Normally armed with six .5 machine-guns, it had a top speed of 475 mph (764 kph) and could fly as high as 42,000 feet (12,801 m).

Churchill Crocodile
This was among the best-known of the armoured division's 'funnies'. This tank could spit out a jet of burning fuel to clear out enemy positions 40–50 yards ahead of it.

17 pounder anti-tank gun

This was the best Allied anti-tank gun of the war, capable of penetrating 149 mm armour at 100 yards.

DUKW (Duplex-Drive amphibious truck)

Known as the 'Duck', this amphibious vehicle could operate on land and sea.

PIAT (Projector Infantry anti-tank)

A hand-held anti-tank weapon, which at close quarters could disable a tank.

Bazooka

An American infantry anti-tank weapon.

Bren Gun

.303 light machine-gun widely used in the British army.

ESCAPE FROM ARNHEM

BATTLE BRIEFING

Two weeks after the Allied landings in France in June 1944, a bridgehead of sixty miles had been secured along the Normandy coastline. But due to skilful German defence the breakout from Normandy was painfully slow. At the end of July, however, the Americans succeeded in smashing through the German lines and poured into the rest of France, whilst the British army broke through at Caen and fought their way into southern Holland.

The Allies were now poised along the river Rhine at the borders of Germany itself. One big push and the war could be brought to an end. But the Germans, though reeling before the attacks, were now more ferocious in defence of their homeland. The Dutch countryside was flooded by Germans to slow down the Allied advance. Furthermore, the British and the Americans were far in advance of their supply lines.

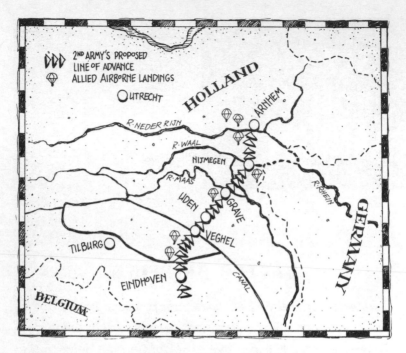

Montgomery's plan for Operation Market Garden.

If only, the Allied generals thought, they could snatch the bridges across the Rhine, then they could drive into the heart of Germany and bring the war in Europe to a quick end.

General Montgomery came up with a bold plan. He would land a '60-mile carpet' of airborne troops behind enemy lines. They would secure all the bridges for the Allies to cross, including the one farthest away which crossed the Rhine itself, at the town of Arnhem. It seemed a dazzling opportunity and the go-ahead was given for the plan to be put into effect.

Parachute drop over Arnhem.

*But it all went horribly wrong. The Germans were waiting,
and waiting in strength. British troops were surrounded and
killed or captured after heroic stands. A few stragglers
attempted the impossible – to escape back to the Allied*

lines. One such soldier was Colonel Graeme Warrack, a doctor with the 1st Airborne Division at Arnhem.

Date: September 1944
Place: Appledoorn hospital barracks, near Arnhem, Holland

In Hiding

There was nothing for it. Doctor Graeme Warrack, Colonel with the 1st Airborne Division, decided that his first duty was to look after the wounded. These men he was now in charge of were all that was left from the force of 10,000 British soldiers dropped or landed sixty miles behind German lines to capture key bridges. True, over 2,000 had escaped back to the British lines, but the

Aerial view of the bridge at Arnhem.

British troops fighting in the rubble of Arnhem.

slaughter had been terrible. Only 600 had made it to the
farthest bridge at Arnhem. Most had never even seen
the bridge at all but had been trapped in a couple of
square miles where they were shot to pieces by German
machine-guns and tanks.

Armed with the only the lightest of weapons, they had
fought against 60-ton Tiger tanks until forced to continue the fight from the cellars of shattered houses.
Hungry and weary, they fought to the last man or, as

they ran out of ammunition, grudgingly surrendered. It had been a gamble to end the war swiftly but it was a risk that hadn't paid off.

Now the survivors were prisoners of the Germans and as Graeme tended the injured his mind turned to thoughts of escape. Once the sick were well enough to be transported to prison camps in Germany he was determined to make a run for it. He was not alone. Many of the other doctors and less seriously injured were hatching escape plans too. It was only 40 kilometres to the front line, although the route was crawling with German soldiers and anyone escaping was likely to be shot. But no one wanted to spend the rest of the war rotting in a prison camp.

Each day more and more British soldiers, as soon as they felt well enough to make a bid for freedom, disappeared from the hospital wards. Hiding in bushes, hayricks and outhouses, they waited until dark and then slipped off into the surrounding countryside.

Unfortunately, Graeme had few advantages as an escapee. He was the senior medical officer and would be missed immediately. He was also very tall – over six foot – and therefore easy to spot. He decided that his only chance was to go into hiding and wait for the British advance to free him.

Graeme searched every nook and cranny of the hospital until, one morning before he began his ward rounds, he sat staring at the ceiling, wondering where he could hide. And then it became blindingly obvious to him. In the rambling warren of the hospital there were bound to be twists, turns and corners in the roof space where he might remain undiscovered.

Once the idea was fixed in his head it didn't take him long to find a hatch in the ceiling near his office. In the days that followed, he stocked the roof space above his office with water, food, blankets, candles and civilian clothing until there were enough provisions to last a long wait.

In October, Graeme waved goodbye to the last of the soldiers who were now well enough to be taken to prison of war camps in Germany. He turned back to the hospital, climbed the stairs to his office and made straight for the trapdoor. Glancing round the office to make sure he'd not been seen, he slid the hatch shut and plunged himself into the gloom and dust of the loft. He would not have a long wait, he thought, for he could already hear the boom of artillery guns a little way to the south. And, with luck, the Germans may think he had been evacuated with the rest of the wounded.

But the Allies didn't arrive. Days turned into weeks. The Germans dynamited canals, making it difficult for the Allies to advance across waterlogged fields. Meanwhile, Graeme was running out of food and water. Terrified that a wrong footfall or a sudden uncontrollable sneeze would betray his presence, he decided that he would have to leave his hiding place.

On 29 October Graeme Warrack opened the hatch of his cramped hiding place. It was a brilliantly moonlit night. He tried to keep to the deep shadows as he edged his way down the stairs to the courtyard below. At first he could barely move his legs. He'd had no exercise cooped up in the tiny roof space. Reaching the lower floor, Graeme glanced through the office window. There appeared to be no sentry on duty outside. He eased the catch free and slowly swung the window open when, to his horror, he caught sight of the shadow of a German soldier less than a metre from him. Graeme was fortunate that the guard had his back to him – this was the probable reason he had not been heard.

Graeme slunk back into the shadows and dropped to the floor below the window. Straining his ears to the utmost, he heard the guard rub his hands for warmth against the frosty night air. Less than a minute later the man stamped his feet and marched off into the night. Graeme could hear his heart pounding in his chest. That had been too close to bear. He blew out a gasp of relief.

Gradually, the guard's footsteps faded into the night. When he could hear them no more, Graeme eased himself up to the window ledge and then cautiously peered out. The guard was 20 metres away and about to turn a corner. That would be his moment to dash across the courtyard.

A small cloud scudded across the moon and plunged the courtyard into darkness. Graeme swung his stiff legs over the sill and gently pushed the window shut behind him. He had only seconds to cross the rain-soaked courtyard before the moon would illuminate everything again. He checked the guard had disappeared and then sprinted across the clearing. But the cobbles were slippery from the rain and as he neared the shadows on the far side of the courtyard between two buildings his feet slid from beneath him. He began to topple backwards but saved himself from clattering to the ground by grasping at a metal railing.

Pausing for breath, he listened for signs that he had been discovered. He expected a guard to come running at any moment, gun blazing. But there was not a sound. So far so good. Graeme studied the way ahead. A further 30 metres would take him to the next deep shadow, close by the stable. Again, he waited until a cloud blotted out the moonlight before dashing across the rest of the courtyard. Pressing himself against the wall, he accidentally scraped the lower masonry with his boot. The sound was barely audible but to him it felt like a thunderclap. Inside the stable, a horse whinnied and shook its head, rattling its halter.

Graeme was sure the noise from the horse would arouse the Germans' suspicions. He screwed his eyes tightly shut. But the noise had gone unnoticed. Opening his eyes, he could now see that he was only metres away from the fence that surrounded the hospital grounds. Beyond was freedom, but also danger.

Graeme felt his way along the fence, searching for a way under or over. The top had been renewed with razor-sharp wire, so Graeme concentrated on finding a slack piece of fence which might allow him to slide underneath. But there seemed no easy way through. Desperation welled up inside him.

Dropping on to his hands and knees, Graeme crawled along the grassy embankment until he came to a clump of trees and bushes, through which the fence ran. He noticed that the roots of one of the trees had grown through the soil and formed a ridge which had bent the bottom of the fence upward. This must not have been so apparent when the wire had been strung in the summer but now that the shrubbery was dying back the roots had pushed the wire up by about 18 centimetres above the ground.

'Just as well I've been on a diet,' Graeme mused to himself. Wriggling on his back, he cleared the wire. Clear of the hospital, his fear returned. This was only the first step in his escape bid. It would be a long and dangerous trek to the Rhine.

In the dark it was easy to get lost but he knew if he could find his way to the railway line at Eade, this would guide him south to the Allied lines. The railway track lay some 18 kilometres away and this would be the next hazardous part of his journey. He had heard that a group of British paratroopers were hiding out there and if he could make it to them, then they all stood a chance of crossing the Rhine to their own side.

Graeme walked through the night and then hid in a small wood at daybreak. The sudden forced activity of the night before, after weeks in his cramped hiding place, made his legs ache. As he lay in his nest of fallen autumn leaves a sudden downpour soaked him to the skin. His lips chattered uncontrollably and he tugged his jacket tightly round his body to keep warm.

A Stroke of Good Luck

As night fell, Graeme set off once more. He was desperately thirsty. He plucked frost-covered oak leaves from the trees and sucked them to quench his thirst.

Deep into the night, he came across a farmhouse. He knew he needed help but contact with anyone was dangerous, even with the Dutch. Some might help, others might hand him in. Most would just tell him to clear off. Anyone caught helping British soldiers was likely to be shot on the spot.

Graeme made his way along a garden fence until he came to a gap in the hedge, where he could see a cottage about 30 metres away. A warm pool of light bathed a patch of garden beneath the window. In the cold, bleak night it seemed so inviting, so irresistible. He decided to risk it and hoped that the people inside would be friendly.

Creeping to the window, Graeme peered in. Two Dutch women were sitting at a kitchen table. Graeme tapped on the window, trying not to panic them. Three short taps, concluded by one long one. Everyone in occupied Europe knew what this meant. It was Morse code – V for victory, used by the BBC as the signature for their broadcasting services to the people of Europe.

Graeme had struck lucky. The Reint family had contacts with the Resistance.

Nevertheless, Tineke Reint was startled when she opened the door. After weeks of cramped confinement, Graeme Warrack looked more like a tramp than a colonel from an elite paratroop regiment. Unshaven, shrouded in a blanket and with a dirt-streaked face and red-rimmed eyes, he looked like a criminal on the run. Tineke would have had just cause to slam the door in his face. But what caught the Dutch partisan's gaze was the red paratrooper's beret that Graeme had deliberately worn so as not to be shot as a spy.

'Come, come quickly.' Tineke shepherded Graeme in as she quickly scanned the neighbourhood to make sure they had not been seen. 'Sit,' Tineke commanded Graeme in the little English she knew. 'Eat.'

After a simple meal, which the starving Dutch could barely provide, Graeme was taken into the woods nearby and hidden in an underground dugout lined with logs. After living in his cramped prison for so long it was a luxury to be able to stretch his legs. That night he slept soundly, feeling warm and safe for the first time in many months.

Familiar and reassuring sounds filtered into his hide-out. The low hum of cars that passed on the nearby road, the chatter of couples walking through the woods. All these sounds gave him a sense of well-being. But as the days passed he became increasingly anxious, not just for his own safety but for that of the Reint family. If caught, the Germans would show no mercy. The men in the family would be shot immediately and the women dragged off to concentration camps.

The Visitor

Graeme's nerves were becoming increasingly frayed. About two weeks after he'd arrived there, as he lay in the straw a sliver of light pierced the gloom, sending a whirl of dust motes dancing in the pale autumn light. A shadow slipped into the dugout, holding a finger to his lips.

'Good evening, Colonel Warrack. I am Piet von Arnhem. I am pleased to say that you will be going home. You will be joining some of your comrades soon and be taken across the river Ede to your friends.'

Graeme felt a huge weight had been lifted from his shoulders. But as the excitement surged through his body at the thought of escape, his fear returned.

'But what of the enemy patrols? We'll be like sitting ducks.'

Piet looked puzzled, not understanding the term 'sitting ducks'.

'The Germans will spot us easily on the water,' Graeme explained.

'No, Colonel. Your soldiers are crossing the river on daring raids almost every night. A short while ago 150 men were helped across to their own lines in this way.' Piet tried to reassure Graeme and sounded very confident, but Graeme was riddled with doubts.

Another Night Escape

Graeme pressed his face to the earth in a shallow ditch whilst bullets whined overhead and thudded into the soft earth by his feet. He could hear grunts and cries of pain from fallen comrades. Sten guns stuttered; grenades exploded, sending showers of earth down on his head.

The carefully laid plan for their mass escape had fallen apart. The Germans were everywhere. One or two men were killed, several wounded and only seven men had made it across the Rhine. Graeme was not one of them.

He wormed his way on his stomach into a nearby clump of trees as the noise of the pursuing Germans grew fainter. They were focusing on the river where some men had attempted a crossing. Graeme darted from bush to bush and as he left the riverbank, the commotion grew fainter and fainter.

There was nothing else left to do but to make his way back to the Reints. He made it safely and joined an American pilot and a Dutch civilian in the familiar underground dugout.

Free At Last

In the first week of February, more than three months after his escape from the hospital at Appledoorn,

Warrack stepped into a wobbling canoe with two Dutch companions. Their plan was to paddle some 20 kilometres down canals and tributaries until they could cross the Rhine. The whole area bristled with defences. Machine-gun posts lay hidden along the riverbanks, searchlights swept the river.

The last stage of the journey was the most terrifying. By this time they were down to one canoe, the others having sunk after becoming waterlogged. A strong wind had whipped up waves and they were only making slow headway.

As they paddled, Graeme's hands had become increasingly bloodied with the effort. His blisters had burst and the tender skin beneath was soon beaded with blood. But they'd gone too far to turn back. As they drifted down a narrow stream a voice barked out, 'Halt! Who goes there?'

The voice was – yes – the voice was speaking English. They'd made it!

FIGHTING FACTS

A Bridge Too Far?

Field Marshall Bernard Montgomery, the hero of El Alamein, was convinced that the war could be brought quickly to an end if the Allied forces could capture the bridges through Holland and over the Rhine into

The bridge at Arnhem.

Germany. The US 101 were to capture the Sindhoven and Uden canal bridges, whilst the US 82 was to take the Maas and Waal bridges.

Most dangerous of all, the British 1st Airborne Division were to be dropped 60 miles behind the enemy lines at a little town called Arnhem, deep inside enemy-held territory.

Montgomery's Deputy-Commander, Lieutenant General 'Boy' Browning, however, thought the plan too risky and warned Montgomery, 'I think we may be going one bridge too far.' He was right.

Dutch Underground Resistance

The Reint family was one among many Dutch people who formed resistance groups after their country's defeat in 1940. Like other resistors in occupied countries they organized sabotage against the hated enemy and sent valuable information about German troop movements to Britain.

Unfortunately, the Germans were lucky enough to capture a radio transmitter and codes in 1941. Sending fake messages to British Intelligence they lured some supplies and agents straight into their hands. After this disaster British Intelligence became very suspicious of any information they received from Holland. It was to prove their undoing at Arnhem. Despite repeated warnings from the Dutch resistance that German panzer divisions were stationed near Arnhem, Montgomery refused to call a halt to his operation.

Caught in the Crossfire

Many civilians were caught up in the middle of the fighting. Private Tucker of the Parachute regiment described one tough old lady who refused to budge from her house:

> We hadn't got far when this young soldier came rushing in to say that there was an old lady in one of the back bedrooms and she was refusing to go. In the end she stayed and the young soldier risked his life a dozen times to feed her. All through the terrible fighting to come, she remained in that back bedroom never turning a hair when all the shells were crashing all around us. Astounded by her courage, it was only

*afterwards that I learned she'd been deaf as a post
all along.*

Escape

Exhausted, hungry and attacked on all sides by flame-throwers and tanks, the parachute regiment hung on to their positions on the bridge at Arnhem for eight days before surrendering to the Germans. Survivors split up into small groups and set out along different routes to make their way back to the British lines.

> *Our major was an old hand. He led the way and linked
> the party together by getting everyone to hold the tail
> of the parachutist's smock of the man in front of him
> so our column resembled some children's game. The
> worst moment was waiting by the riverside (Lower
> Rhine) till our turn came to be ferried across. The
> Germans kept sending up flares and we had to lie flat
> and motionless on a soaking field with cold rain
> drizzling down.*

Was Arnhem a Success?

The Allies claimed it was because they had captured a number of bridges through Holland. However, they had failed to hang on to the bridge at Arnhem. This was vital to the 'dagger thrust' at Germany.

Once the airborne troops had landed the Germans knew to concentrate their counter-attack along the route attempted by the relieving second army. The

Sherman tanks went to the aid of the British forces but they were sitting targets as they travelled through the flat Dutch countryside on the raised roads.

THE BATTLE FOR BURMA

BATTLE BRIEFING

The Japanese menace had been steadily growing in the Far East throughout the 1930s. Dominated by the army, the Japanese government was forced to accept the imperial ambitions of its generals. Most of China fell to their military forces and they looked to expand their empire further by grabbing the colonies of the French and British in the Far East. After 1940 only the United States stood in their way, for Britain was fighting for her own survival and France had been defeated by Germany.

Whilst discussions were taking place between Japan and America, the Japanese launched a massive surprise attack on the American naval base at Pearl Harbor in Hawaii on 7 December 1941. Three hundred and fifty-three Japanese planes, launched from six aircraft carriers, destroyed six battleships, three cruisers, three destroyers and 149 planes.

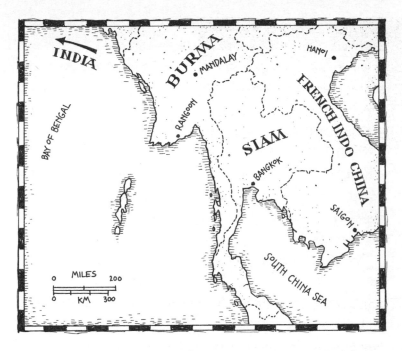

Burma.

Over 4,000 American soldiers and civilians were killed or wounded in the raid. The American Pacific fleet was all but paralysed. Left with only the shattered remnants of a fleet to oppose them, the Japanese were free to spread across the Asian mainland and the Pacific.

As a result of the attack on Pearl Harbor, the USA officially declared war on Japan on 10 December 1941. Then Germany and Italy, Japan's allies, declared war on the USA. What had been mainly a European war had now truly become a world war.

The Japanese lost little time in attacking the British Empire in the Far East. On 11 December 1941 Malaya was invaded. Four days later, Japanese troops invaded Burma, with the intention of sweeping on to India, the 'jewel' of the British Empire.

The British were in a perilous position. Not only had they lost vast areas of their empire to the Japanese but also many Indian subjects were demanding independence from Britain. For this reason, the loyalty of thousands of Indians who served in the British Indian army could now no longer be taken for granted.

The British position became even more desperate. On 15 February 1942, the great British naval base at Singapore fell to Japanese forces. There seemed little that could be done to stop the advancing tide. Throughout early 1942 the Imperial Japanese armies made a series of rapid gains. They captured many of the islands across the western Pacific and even threatened Australia itself. By 20 May 1942 all of Burma was in Japanese hands and they were poised to strike into India.

The British decided to try and hold the frontier fast, whilst sending guerrilla troops to fight deep inside enemy territory. By the end of the year, after fierce fighting, the Allies began to win the struggle against the Japanese. By May 1945, Rangoon, the capital of Burma, was recaptured. In the Pacific, American and Allied forces retook Japanese-held islands. The cost of these campaigns in human life was huge.

In order to end the war quickly and save the lives of further Allied soldiers, it was decided to use a secret weapon. On

6 August 1945 an atom bomb was dropped on the town of Hiroshima in Japan, causing thousands of deaths and injuries. After a second atomic bomb was used on Nagasaki, the Japanese surrendered on 14 August 1945.

Most attention was focused on the war in Europe, and so many of the soldiers who fought in the Allied armies in the Far East have come to regard themselves as the 'Forgotten Army'. One such man was Martin McLane. What is frequently forgotten as well is that many of the soldiers came from many different parts of the world – from Africa, the West Indies and from India itself. Rifleman Lachhiman Gurung was one such soldier. Born in Nepal, he came from a long line of people who had fought courageously in the British Army.

The Forgotten Army

The Meeting

The Royal Chelsea Hospital sits near the banks of the River Thames in London. Strictly speaking it isn't a hospital at all but a home for retired soldiers built by Charles II over three hundred years ago. And so it remains today – much larger than when it was first built, but still carrying on the traditions of the past. There are over 700 pensioners in the Royal Hospital, each one with a fascinating story to tell. Many are in their eighties and nineties and when they pass away, their stories will be lost, their histories forgotten.

I first came across Martin McLane, one of the pensioners, in a magazine article about the war in Burma. Martin's photograph was also there. Taken during World War II, the faded and dog-eared picture showed a stocky, well-built man. His hair was neatly groomed and a broad wave of moustache swept across his upper lip. The mouth gave a hint of a smile. But it was his eyes that caught my attention. They positively glittered with humour and intelligence. After an exchange of letters, I arranged to meet Martin.

After lunch Martin and I sat back in two comfortable armchairs. Resting his walking stick against the arm of the chair, he folded his hands together and began.

'So you want to hear about Burma. Well, there'll be things I'll tell you that you won't find in the history books.'

Setting Off

France and the retreat to Dunkirk was bad enough but there was worse to come when the Japanese began to attack us in the East and the 2nd battalion was given orders for overseas. We embarked on a troop train and were under strict orders not to leave the carriages. On 12 April, my birthday, we embarked on the *Empress of Canada*, a cruise liner converted to a troopship.

We steamed well out into the Atlantic to stay clear of submarines, and were escorted by destroyers and cruisers. The Mediterranean was too dangerous so we had to go right round Africa. What a welcome as we rounded the Cape. The docks of Capetown were lined with women singing a greeting and we were allowed four hours' leave.

Now Pat Brennan, my best friend, loved to gamble but he had no money. 'Lend me a few bob, Martin. There's a game going on over there.'

Of course, he lost everything, but he was a mate so there was no bad feeling. Years later Pat became an officer and we were still the best of friends, went everywhere together until we were both called into the commander's office one day and told the friendship had to end. You see, officers and men couldn't mix together socially. I didn't like it but that was the army. I guess they were afraid it would confuse everybody. You had to keep your distance.

You can imagine the next morning everyone was late back. They'd had such a good time ashore. Our thoughts began to turn to our destination. We still didn't know where it would be. That was a secret. If the enemy found out, the ship could have been sunk. But we had a pretty good idea. Singapore – the rumour spread around the ship. We knew the Japs had their eyes on the place. But we were wrong. Singapore fell and we arrived in India instead.

Into Battle

We weren't very welcome there. Many Indians were followers of Mahatma Gandhi who wanted the British to 'quit India' and for India to win her independence after being a British colony for nearly two hundred years.

Our job, as it gradually became clear, was to be

103

trained in jungle warfare. I'll tell you, the jungle is a frightening place. No sun penetrates so there's little light. The vegetation is thick and you never know where the enemy might be lying in wait for you. The Japanese, on the other hand, had adapted well. They'd built bunkers, covered with huge logs and earth. They could live on a handful of rice and were fanatical in attack; happy to lose their lives for their country.

Our soldiers were tough but even the best can be let down if they haven't the right equipment. For example, when we went into battle, we wore khaki Drill Battle Dress. It was sandy-coloured and quite unfit for jungle camouflage where we stood out distinctively. No effort was made to alter this. We even wore white vests and underwear, which meant if you took your tunic off, you became even more prominent against the dark greens of the jungle.

Just imagine the state we were in after six weeks of fighting in battle or lying in holes in the ground for pro-tection. We did have one spare kit but this was lost when the Japs overran Brigade Headquarters where they were stored. We also couldn't take hot showers when we were front-line troops. All we could do was use part of our water ration for washing. If we felt really scruffy, we'd pour some water into our mess tins, the same tin that we used for meals, and try to wash and shave in it. We must have stunk. It's surprising the Japs couldn't smell us coming!

Worse than the lack of proper camouflaged uniforms were the faulty weapons we were given. We'd been issued with a new type of Thompson sub-machine-gun and the men were keen to get their hands on what they thought was going to be a much better weapon. As a Company Sergeant Major – I'd been promoted by this time – I was due to get one but no instructions came with them.

'McLane,' the Company Commander barked, 'bring me my Thompson. I want to try it out.'

I handed him the weapon and we went down to the beach together so he could fire it into the sea. Steadying the gun against his hip, he let off one round. I looked in the direction it should have gone but couldn't spot the plume of water it should have made.

'Stop, sir!' I held my hand up. 'I don't like the sound of that shot.' It had sounded muffled.

'You're too cautious,' he replied. 'It's a new gun. Sounds different.'

He took aim once more and squeezed the trigger. BANG! My ears rang from the sound as I realized that the first round had stuck in the barrel. The second round hadn't a clear passage and the gun had burst apart. The Commander reeled back with the force of the explosion and fell to the ground unconscious. I dropped to my knees and scanned his body for wounds. Amazingly there were none. Gradually, his eyes flickered open and a few moments later he began to remember what had happened.

The army doesn't like to admit mistakes and the faulty Thompson machine-gun was said to be a freak and the others were fine. Yet no one was allowed to test them — with disastrous results, as I'll tell you.

The Attack

The officers decided that they would put in an attack on the Japanese positions. The sea was to our right whilst we were dug in flat lands partly covered by jungle. Immediately in front of our position were three dried-up river beds, carved out of the soft soil on the seaward side by the heavy monsoon rains. We couldn't outflank the Japanese and so had to meet them head on.

We had a special commando group in our battalion who went in first under cover of darkness. They were to cross a tidal river or *chung* down by the beach. They all had Thompson machine-guns, rifles and grenades and their faces were blackened.

I was detailed to the observation post in the front line to listen to the attack and judge how it was going. After a few moments I heard the thump of the grenades but I couldn't hear the rattle of automatic fire from the Thompsons. All of a sudden, the commando group came crashing back through the jungle, cursing and swearing. It was the Thompsons. They'd let us down again.

This was serious but it was wartime and there was no enquiry in case the soldiers lost confidence in their weapons. Well, we had no confidence at all. The army blamed the ammunition. Some said the American ammunition we were given wasn't waterproof. Others said it had been tampered with by anti-British Indians.

The attack was called off until new ammunition arrived but when it arrived it looked poor quality. Cheap, thin bright brass casings instead of bronze. Again our guns failed when we went into attack. It made me cry to see those brave young conscripts shattered by shrapnel. But I was told to press on with the attack. If the guns were defective then we were to use grenades. The carnage was terrible. Major Hurtman had been shot in the knee and couldn't move so I carried him to safety. I looked hard but there seemed to be no officer left unwounded and so I found myself in charge.

I decided to lead the men out, and all the time the Commanding Officer was complaining that we hadn't fought hard enough. But there were only fifteen men left out of a company of 90. The attack was a failure and there was no point in leading men to their deaths when all was hopeless.

Now, I've seen history books describe our efforts as weak-kneed but they weren't there. They don't understand that the monsoons had gouged the banks of the dried riverbeds until they were impossible to scale without ladders. Even then we had to carry 70 lb packs on our backs. Nor could we rely on our weapons or the ammunition. No, the battle in the Arakan was lost, not by the men but by faulty weapons and bad planning. But you don't always hear the history from the soldiers who fought the battles.

Rifleman Lachhiman Gurung VC
Date: 12/13 May 1945
Place: Taungdawn, the Irrawaddy River, Burma

A Proud Day

Rifleman Lachhiman Gurung stood to attention, trying to stand taller than his modest five feet. The sun was beating down on the parade ground at the Red Fort, Delhi, and although he'd stood to attention for well over an hour it didn't matter to him. Ringing the central square, regiments of the British Indian army and the British army stood rigidly in line. Brilliant red, green and gold flags fluttered alongside Union Jacks; cavalry horses gently pawed the ground or snorted in the heat of the day. It all looked magnificent.

He found it hard to believe but they were here to honour him – a Gurkha from a village deep in the remote Chitwan district of western Nepal. He was soon to be awarded the highest military honour in the British army – the Victoria Cross.

When he looked back over his life in the army he thought how lucky he'd been to get into the services at all due to his height – in peacetime he would have been rejected. But the demands of war and the shortage of soldiers had meant that the British army had had to lower their height standards. What Lachhiman lacked in height, however, he made up for in courage.

Lachhiman had enlisted in 1941, the lowest point in the war for Britain. With Europe under the heel of the Nazis, the Japanese had struck in the Far East. Malaya, Singapore and Burma had fallen and the Imperial Japanese armies were poised on the frontiers of India itself. Lachhiman was thrown into battle alongside Indian, British, East and West African, and Burmese soldiers in a desperate attempt to stem the tide of the Japanese advance.

But although the Japanese had been victorious, their supply lines were badly over-stretched and their attacks began to falter. But not before both sides had experienced some of the most bitter fighting of the war at the two Indian border stations of Imphal and Kohima. So close were the two armies at one point that at night, it was just possible to hear enemy troops breathing only a few feet away.

Behind the Japanese lines, Allied troops deep in Japanese-held land were causing havoc and devastation to railways and roads supplying the Japanese forces. The Japanese had no choice but to retreat. It had been a close fight. If the Japanese had broken through at Kohima then they could have flooded on to the plains of India and possibly linked-up with the German armies in the Caucasus in Russia.

But the battles on the borders of India had been deci-

A soldier covers his comrades
with a Bren Gun.

sive. The war was not over but it was the beginning of
the end for the Japanese Imperial armies.

A History of Heroes

Lachhiman came from a people who had always been
fighters. First recruited into the British army during the
reign of Queen Victoria in the mid-nineteenth century,
they earned a well-deserved reputation as loyal and
ferocious fighters. Born in remote villages of the
Himalayas in the kingdom of Nepal, they knew how to
survive under the most difficult conditions. Lachhiman
himself came from a long line of volunteers who had

served the British Empire and he wished to be part of the same tradition.

In March 1945 Lachhiman was posted to the 4th Battalion, 8th Gurkha Rifles in Burma. By May the Japanese forces were retreating down the Irrawaddy River that runs the whole length of the country. The jungle, swamp and mountain ranges of Burma were formidable obstacles in themselves. Dense foliage gave perfect cover for ambushes and meant every foot of land had to be hacked through. Nor would the Japanese give up

Ghurka soldiers after a battle with the
Japanese, on Linch Hill.

ground easily, sacrificing hundreds of men to delay the enemy advance. Each of their soldiers had a fanatical belief in their Emperor and was willing to die for him. The worst humiliation for a Japanese soldier was to be defeated and taken prisoner, for this brought shame on the man's family as well as himself. This explains why they fought so ferociously, with little regard for their own lives, and why they were often cruel to the prisoners they captured.

Stand and Fight

On 11 May, 'B' and 'C' Companies in Lachhiman's battalion were ordered to hold an important position astride a forest track on the west side of the river near to the village of Taungdaw. This track was vital to the Japanese breakout. Many of them had been cut off and were desperately trying to break through to escape capture. For three days and nights the Japanese launched attack after attack at British positions. But against well dug-in positions the Japanese attempts were suicidal and the hillside was soon littered with their dead. Again and again, they threw themselves across the clearings, only to be mown down by machine-guns.

The key position was held by No. 9 platoon almost 100 yards (91 m) forward of the remainder of the company. They were bearing the brunt of the attack. And in the most exposed position of all was Lachhiman's section. They were ordered to hold the line at all costs. They expected attacks at any time and all the time. Their nerves were taut and they scanned the undergrowth for any movement that might erupt into an attack.

The Japanese had switched their attacks to night in an attempt to both reduce casualties and to take the British by surprise. There was no moonlight to speak of and every rustle of bush and screech of animal grated the British soldiers' nerves.

At 1:20 in the morning about 200 enemy soldiers assaulted Lachhiman's section and he was in the front

A Gurkha soldier carries a wounded comrade
from the battlefield.

line. He understood well that if his trench were overrun it would open up the track behind him. This would allow the enemy to break through and overwhelm the rest of the two companies dug in along the hillside.

Lachhiman kept up a constant fire, stopping only once when a grenade bounced on the lip of his trench. He at once grasped the bomb and hurled it back in the direction of the enemy. No sooner had he done so than another landed in the trench at his feet. He picked this one up too and threw it back at the enemy.

The grenades fragmented in a blinding explosion. Screams of men in agony tore the night apart, but he had achieved his objective. Most of the Japanese in the vanguard of the attack had been killed.

Lacchiman slowly raised his eyes above the lip of the trench, only to see a third grenade bouncing towards him, only two feet away. As enemy bullets whined about his head, he reached out and took the grenade in his hand, stretching his arm back to throw it at the enemy when it exploded in his grasp. Lachhiman reeled back into the trench, his head pounding with the noise of the explosion. He could see that where his fingers should have been there was now only a bloody stump. Nor could he move his arm, which hung limp at his side. Because he'd been in a trench much of the explosion had also caught him in the face and streams of blood clouded his vision. For a brief moment he thought his life would soon come to an end.

He looked round for his two comrades but quickly realized that neither of them would be able to help him. Both had been badly wounded and lay writhing in agony at the bottom of the trench.

Lachhiman struggled to his feet and wiped the blood from his face with the back of his hand. He could feel only numbness in his right hand and arm, for the pain of his injuries had not begun to bite into his mind.

At the edge of the clearing, beyond the mounds of dead, the enemy were forming up again, shoulder to shoulder, for what seemed to be a final assault. Sheer weight of numbers would easily overrun Lachhiman's position and he could expect little help from the hard-pressed remainder of his section.

Rifleman Lachhiman Gurung steadied himself. He ignored his wounds and calmly but quickly began to reload his rifle with his left hand. Firing volley after volley, he kept up a steady and continuous rate of fire. Screaming and shouting, the Japanese lines faltered and then failed. They regrouped and charged again but nothing could unnerve Lachhiman as he kept up a hail of fire on the attacking, screaming hordes.

The Death Toll Mounts

Incredibly, Lachhiman stayed at his post for four hours, pouring a constant stream of fire on the enemy. The severely wounded rifleman propped himself up and calmly waited for each renewed attack, which he met with fire at point-blank range. He was determined that he would not give one inch of ground for the honour of his platoon and his ancestors.

The attack began to peter out after that, for even the Japanese could not endure such heavy losses and he heard them retreat through the undergrowth. He slumped back into the trench, barely able to stand after his constant efforts and from the loss of blood. He heard friendly voices as his head began to swim and he lost unconsciousness.

His rescuers could hardly believe their eyes. Eighty-seven enemy dead lay in front of Lachhiman's section, 31 of which lay directly in front of his trench. His comrades were in no doubt that the rifleman had saved them all, for had the Japanese overrun his position then the reverse slope would have fallen and the whole company would have been wiped out.

Rifleman Lachhiman Gurung was evacuated to hospital but the surgeons were unable to save his right hand and the use of his right eye. He bore his wounds without complaint and after several weeks in hospital he was fit enough to return to his unit.

The Parade

And now the proudest moment in his life had arrived. The order to stand to attention was bellowed out across the parade ground and every soldier snapped to attention as if one man.

'Rifleman Lachhiman Gurung. Three paces to the front!'

The Gurkha soldier stamped his right foot and marched smartly from the ranks of his comrades, his arms swinging in wide arcs before clattering to a halt and standing stiffly to attention. The broad brim of his hat shielded his eyes from the glare of the sun as a tall British official approached him. This was no less a person than His Excellency, Field Marshall Lord Wavell, the Viceroy who ruled India on behalf of King George VI.

For a brief moment, Lachhiman glanced beyond His Excellency to where his father was sitting on the edge of the parade ground. Too old to walk the distance from his remote village in Nepal, he had been carried for eleven days to be present at the Red Fort ceremony. A small tear gathered at the corner of the old man's eye as the Viceroy pinned the Victoria Cross on his son's chest.

FIGHTING FACTS

What happened to Rifleman Lachhiman Gurung?
Despite the loss of his right hand and eye, Lachhiman continued to serve in the 8th Gurkha Rifles, remaining in India after the country became independent from Britain in 1948. He was promoted to Havildar, the equivalent of a sergeant, but then retired shortly afterwards to his village in Nepal. The tradition of his family serving in the army, however, lived on. To the great

pride of his father, Lachhiman's son also enlisted in the 8th Gurkha Rifles, eventually rising to the rank of officer.

Strengths of British and Japanese units in Burma
British

Army	60,000–100,000
Corps	30,000–50,000 (an army has three corps)
Infantry division	13,700 (a corps has three divisions)
Infantry brigade	2,500 (a division has three brigades)
Infantry company	127 (a battalion has four companies)
Infantry platoon	32 (a company has three platoons)
Infantry section	8 (a platoon has three sections)

A British division's battalions would be entirely British troops. In an Indian division, a third would be British, the rest Indians and Gurkhas.

Japanese
The Japanese division in Burma varied greatly in strength, between 12,000 and 22,000. In total their troops varied between 100,000–120,000.

From All Over the Empire
It is sometimes forgotten that millions of soldiers from India, Pakistan, Bangladesh, Africa and the Caribbean also fought alongside British troops. In World War II around three million people from the Indian sub-conti-

nent joined the Allied war effort, forming the largest volunteer army the world has ever seen. Of the 27 Victoria Crosses awarded during the Burma campaign, members of the Indian armed services won 20. Several thousand people from the Caribbean also served, as did 375,000 Africans.

At last they are to be recognized. A set of commemorative gates will be set up in the near future near to Buckingham Palace – as a constant reminder of their bravery and sacrifice.

Orde Wingate

Orde Wingate was a British soldier who had first made a name for himself leading Jewish fighters against Arab rebels in Palestine in 1936. He put forward the idea of sending forces deep behind Japanese lines so that they could launch unexpected attacks. His guerrilla soldiers were called 'Chindits' and the first force of 3,000 proved so successful that his army was expanded to 12,000.

They were kept supplied from airdrops but if any were wounded they had to be left behind and take their luck in being captured. Wingate himself was killed in an air crash on 24 March 1944.

Not likely!

The Chindits would disappear into the jungle for months at a time and, to prevent their families worrying, an officer was given the job of writing postcards back to their homes. The officer would write that, 'at the end of the operation he will write home as usual'. One angry mother complained bitterly. What did they mean 'as usual'? She hadn't heard from her son for three years!

GLOSSARY

Bren gun – a lightweight quick-firing machine-gun
Gurkha – a Nepalese soldier serving in the British army
Luftwaffe – the German air force
Panzer – armoured troops or a German tank
Partisan – a guerrilla fighter, loyal to a cause
PIAT (Projector Infantry anti-tank) – a hand-held anti-tank
    weapon, which at close quarters could disable a tank
Sten gun – a type of lightweight sub-machine-gun

ACKNOWLEDGEMENTS

Imperial War Museum: p.22 FX7529, p.23 LD305, p.30 EI3465, p.35 EI8493, p.54 MH27176, p.56 HU49815, p.62 B5013, p.64 B5114, p.67 B5055, p.77 BU1024, p.82 MH2061, p.94 HU2127, p.110 IND3479, p.111 IND3616, p.113 IB283; AKG Photo: p.57 2–G56–W3–1941–25; Robert Hunt Library: p.73, p.77 CL1169, p.83.

Every effort has been made to trace copyright holders. We would be grateful to hear from any copyright holders not acknowledged here.

Townley Grammar School for Girls
Townley Road, Bexleyheath, Kent DA6 7AB